Belief Systems *and* Supernaturalism *of* Thachanadan Moopan *of* Wayanad: Changing Trends *and* Persisting Traditions

BELIEF SYSTEMS *and* SUPERNATURALISM *of* THACHANADAN MOOPAN *of* WAYANAD: CHANGING TRENDS *and* PERSISTING TRADITIONS

Sreejisha V P

PARTRIDGE

A Penguin Random House Company

To order additional copies of this book, contact
Partridge India
000 800 10062 62
orders.india@partridgepublishing.com

www.partridgepublishing.com/india

Acknowledgement

From the depth of my heart I express my deep sincere gratitude to the Almighty for his blessings he has bestowed upon me to do this work. Therefore I am indebted to my M Phil guide and supervisor **Dr. Jesurathnam Devarapalli**, *Assistant Professor, Dept. of Anthropology, Pondicherry University. I am grateful for his kind consideration, timely help and scholarly suggestions throughout the course. He refined the thoughts and ideas and put his valuable suggestions to bring this dissertation to its desired form. I thank him deeply for the help and guidance, which I received from him at every stage of my work.*

I am also thanking full to all **Thachanadan Moopan members** *for their co-operation, sharing of knowledge and help during my field work.*

I thank UGC and Pondicherry University for awarding monthly fellowship during the course of M. Phil work.

I am sincerely thankful to Mr. Ramanunni (PEEP), Advt. Priya Satheesh, Mr. Satheesh, Mr. Gireesh, Mr. Subrahmanyam, and Mr. Balakrishnan for their support in the field.

Last, but not least my regards to my parents and brother for their co-operation, encouragement and moral support to me in completing this dissertation work.

PREFACE

Thachanadan Moopan is a scheduled tribe distributed in Wayanad district of Kerala. The present study is conducted mainly in four settlements of Wayanad. The study is focused on traditional belief system among the Thachanadan Moopan with special reference to the changes taking place due to the processes of acculturation, Hinduisation and Christianization. To generate data, the methodological tools utilized are schedule to get quantitative data and interviews, observation, case study and all suitable anthropological technologies to get qualitative data. Traditionally they believe in ancestor spirits. They have their own beliefs, myths, rituals and ceremonies, along with religious and political head. Historically they have their identity and are segregated from other cultures. But now due to the impact of acculturation, Hinduisation and Christianization Thachanadan Moopan absorbing new ideas and customs to their traditional culture. Thus now they are facing an identity problem of Hinduised or Christianized. We should understand the problems they are facing and factors behind these changes in the tribal society. Their culture in its uniqueness is diminishing which may reflective in their changing religious parties.

Sreejisha V P

CONTENTS

1

INTRODUCTION

Religion is a system of belief, which binds humans together and organizing their lives with a specific social and cultural background. Therefore, religion gives an identity to the social group. Accordingly religion offer answers to the questions, which are considered to be beyond themselves, such as ideas, beliefs, supernatural, rituals, etc. The word religion came from the Latin *religare*, which meant 'to bind together' or from the word *religere* which meant 'to rehearse'. The discussion of human beings with supernatural beings is very old and its attributes as a sudden or mysterious happenings or natural disasters akin to draught, famine, sickness and worship or accident etc. It is believed that by propitiating the god or goddess or deity or spirit they can control or reduce the awful situations. These practices are generally called as rituals. Hence religion contains a body of beliefs, values, rituals, objects, etc. Saler states that what explains religious thought or behavior may also explain many other domains of cultural thought and behavior (Boyer 2008:112), the one which explains the religious thought and behavior is nothing but culture from where the notion of right and wrong arises. The notion of right and wrong is the basis for the formation of any structure, which gives rise to any culture. So culture explains each and every aspect which is under its domain. With the time and space the nature and practices of religion changes and its forms are varied.

Anthropological Perspective of Religion

Anthropology defined religion in many ways. E. B. Tylor (1871) defined religion in the simplest words as the belief in spiritual beings. According to Tylor when he discusses about the primitive religion or the forerunners of religion mostly had a belief in spiritual beings which can also interpret as supernatural's. Anthropologists like Durkheim, Weber, Maliknowski and Geertz have their own views regarding religion. Durkhiem views religion in the context of sacred and profane, Maliknowski made a distinction between religion and common sense and Geertz views religion as a cultural dimension of religious analysis. Anthropology views the belief in religion is as they are socialized in that way. Thus socialization had a prominent role belief in religion. Geertz defined religion as a i) a system of symbols which acts to establish powerful, pervasive and long lasting moods and motivations in men by formulating conceptions of a general order of existence and clothing these conceptions with such an aura of factuality that, the moods and motivations seem uniquely realistic. Religion is the belief in the supernatural (Horton 1960:201). Horton state that those things believed by the people are supernatural, which is the base of religion. For any institution there should be some basic requirements to frame the structure, in the case of religion, according to Tylor and Horton supernatural and spiritual beings are the basic structures in the form of religion. Weber (1963:116-7) states that the human motive towards religion is to understand the cosmos, and to be aware of the available natural beings and its relations with him.

Weber's statement about religion is the continuation of Tylor and Horton's statements, as they are discussing about the primitive forms of religion, it evolved from the belief of supernatural to understanding the natural beings. In Spencer's classic formulation of a movement from simple, small scale homogenous to complex, large scale heterogeneous societies, a fairly straight forward parallel could be drawn in the religious field from the simple form of religion of animism, i.e. The worship of many different spirits and sacred powers among primitives through a polytheistic stage to be found in ancient civilizations, to a more complex stage of monotheism, which developed in recent times (Scharf 1970:15). Today neither animism nor animatism is regarded as an earlier, or original or universal form of religion (D'Souza 2005: 56).

Yinger (1957: 95) defined religion as the cultural knowledge that people use to cope with the ultimate problems of human life. Religion is a mechanism identified or created by the human population to escape from certain problems, which they cannot understand or they cannot manage. For example, a fall of rain, as it is a natural happening the earlier population unable to understand what is going on, whether the rain is low or high they seeks the help of their deity to control that, by this the knowledge they gained will be helpful to cope up with the problems they face.

Animism

The first theory on the origin of religion appeared in E.B Tylor's eminent work of Primitive Culture. The Latin word for soul is 'anima' and the theory coined from this belief is called animism (Kottak 1987:511). According to Tylor religion is evolving, when people attempted to understand the conditions and events that could not be explained by daily experiences (Kottak 1987:413). The term animism according to Sahay (1998) was used to describe the exceedingly crude form of religion. Animism characterizes tribes very low in the in the scale of humanity. Animism in its full development, includes the belief in souls, in controlling deities and subordinate spirits, these doctrines practically resulting in some kind of active worship (Tylor 2002:5).

Animatism

Theory of pre-animism or animatism or dynamism introduced by R.R Marrett as a rudimentary form of religion. The dynamism refers to the presence of a power that was not necessarily individualized. He opined that Animatism emerged earlier than animism. And shows the classic example of 'mana' of trobriand islanders, that refers to the supernatural power that influences human.

Manaism

There is another theory regarding the origin of religion. Marrett developed a special form of animatist theory called 'manaism' (Majumdar 1986:134). Marett said that the entire religious life of the primitive is born out of their belief in certain non-understandable, impersonal, non materiel, and non-individualised supernatural power which takes abode in all the objects, animate and inanimate, that exist in the world (Majumdar 1986:134). This impersonal force that exists in the universe and could reside in people, animals, plants and objects was called '*mana*' (Davis 1981:45). It may differ in intensity, the degree in which it is present in a person or an object, but in essence it always the same. Such a set of beliefs Marrett called Animatism or Manaism. The belief of the impersonal force or the supernatural powers vested with every object, whether, animate or inanimate is called as *mana*.

Fetishism

Fetishism is the worship of material objects that were supposed to have an inherent power. A specific power that was believed to reside in a specific object would be set in the operation by the pronouncement of formula that of itself could wield power (Herskovitz 1974:225). Fetishism implied a symbol of a 'supernatural divine' energy which could be harnessed and used (Mesquittela 1983:315).

Totemism

Totemism is associated with supernatural belief that is related to a social division like band or cheifdom. These social divisions represent a certain animal or plant or other natural objects as its origin. Thus the descent of certain tribal groups, traced through the totemic plant or animal. As per the customary rules certain taboos are practiced to prohibit the killing or eating or any other kinds of destruction of such totemic species. Those totems are worshiping with grand ceremonial functions as they are regarded their guardians and they are worn the totemic emblems in body parts or tattooed. Most of the tribal groups are named after the totem.

Naturism

According to Max Muller the earliest form of religion must have been the worship of objects of nature. The best examples of nature worship are the Mal Paharias, who worshipped the sun (*beru*) and earth (*dharthi*). In South India the Todas and Koyas worship sun as their deity.

Polytheism

Polytheism is a form of religion in which the people believe in plural Gods. It is generally considered as the third stage of religious evolution (Srivastava 2008: 208). Polytheism is widely prevalent in the advanced societies, where they worship gods, goddesses, deities and ancestral spirits. It is believed that for Hinduism there are 3,30,00,000 Gods and Goddesses are associated with regional and local variations. The presence of polytheism was widely found among the ancient Greek, Egyptian and Roman cultures.

Monotheism

Monotheism derived from Greek words *mono*, which means 'single' and *theos*, which means 'god'. It is believed that there is only one supreme god and he created the cosmos. It is widely discussed that the first monotheistic religion is Zoroastrianism, which had a certain code of conduct with a holy book named Avesta. It is still in practice in Iran. Monotheism is the widely held idea that the belief in only one God is found among Christianity, Islam and Judaism, which are called Abrahamic religions.

Atheism

Aetheism refers to the absence of belief in God. The term aetheism originated from Greek word *aethos*, which means ''without the gods'. The believers of aetheism had no conception of a god or they are the rationale for the lack of empirical evidence for the existence of a supreme creator.

Supernaturalism

The term nature is originated from the French word 'natura' which means, natural character, from this the term Supernatural evolved. Supernatural refers to 'beyond nature' or 'something more than that of nature'. Therefore, people believe that the supernatural has the power or energy at anywhere and anytime. Belief in the supernatural is mainly found among the primitive communities like Chenchu's of Andhra Pradesh, Kattunaikkan's of Kerala, etc. According to Bagabati (1998:246) religion is any set of attitudes, beliefs and practices pertaining to supernatural powers, whether that power is forces god, spirits, ghosts or demons. The supernatural is generally regarded as a serious subject, but it is also because of the social intimations of the supernatural are also readily taken as departure points for fundamental theories of social order (Wilson 1979:270). Religion in all its forms involves an emotional attitude toward the universe, especially toward the unknown powers or agencies which are believed to be behind its phenomena (Ellwood 1913:294). As Madan (1986) views that the belief in certain understandable, impersonal, non-material and non-individualised supernatural power, which takes abode in all the objects animate and inanimate that exists in the world forms the religious life of the primitive people. But in some case supernatural one found in the personified form as noted by Miller (1999) that some supernatural are the partial shape of animals called zoomorphic deities and some are in the form of human, that are common but not universal i.e. the deceased ancestor called Anthropomorphic supernatural deities. Goode (1951) views in much more broader sense that gods in 'anthropo social' meant to be the social welfare of the group is intended by the supernatural and the supernatural in 'anthropo psychic' implies the moody, loved, concerned, vain nature of the gods. Debnath (2003) discussed about the classification of supernatural beings of the aborigines of India as (1) The Supreme Deity (2) The Village Tutelary Deities (3) Sub clan spirits (4) Household Spirits or Deities (5) Ancestral Spirits (6) Malevolent or Evil Spirits (7) Regional Hindu deities which are borrowed to the tribal religious pantheon. Through various ritualistic activities performed on some occasions such as rituals related to farming, rituals related to eradicate some diseases, etc. the relationship with supernatural world is being maintained.

Birx (2006) defined a religious ritual is a prescribed routinized and ceremonial action or set of actions as well as symbolic and has specific significance to the performer i.e. the shaman or priest and the performer's community. Thus the shamans or priests of each society have their own method of control. In the primitive groups the religious object are not prayer but magic. MacLennan (1922: 605) observes that the religious object cannot properly be appealed to; it can only be manipulated. Sharma (2001) says that ritual behavior is motivated by the desire to gain some form of satisfaction and is expected to be effective and those human concerns are health, fertility and general welfare, etc. As opined by Eller (2007) one familiar form of therapeutic ritual is shamanism. He mentioned the term therapeutic ritual to refer the rituals which are performed to eliminate some diseases. Shamanism was studied by Vitebsley (2001) he states that shaman switch to an altered state of consciousness and conveys the spirit realm. This spirit realm is elaborated by different cultures in different ways. Vitebsley specifying that the trance of a human being in an altered stage of super human is necessary and then only he get the name Shaman. Vidyarthi (1983) noted that in South India most of the tribal groups have a Pujari (Priest) and a Kaviyan, and he performs the main sacred performances and sacrifices to propitiate the god or deity. The supernatural beliefs are highly related to ecological and other factors. Thus the changes in these factors cause changes in the belief system of supernatural also.

Review of literature

Rather than merely an understanding of the existing system or the structure of the religion in the present study focuses on the social perspective with a functional point on the role of religion in the tribal world. Therefore a thick description of the customs and beliefs of the communities must be overview to appraise the causes and consequences of the changes and enriching factors that persisting tradition in the tribal world.

What Anthropology views on religion is explained by MacLennan (1922) that, religion as a fundamental function of the human social order and it varies with the evolution of this social order that its final test must consist in its human service (a) as reflecting the fundamental, effective values of man's life and (b) as also reflecting man's more permanent and intelligent attitudes toward his environment. Seul (1999) views that religions often serve the psychological needs more broadly and potently than other accumulation of cultural meaning that contribute to the construction and maintenance of individual and group identities. Moreover, it supplies cosmologies, moral frameworks, institutions, rituals, traditions, and other identity-supporting content that answers to individuals' needs for psychological stability in the form of a predictable world, a sense of belonging, self- esteem, and even self-actualization. Cornwall (1987) indicates that personal community relationships have the strongest direct influence of belief and commitment, but that religious socialization and demographic characteristics influence religious belief and commitment indirectly because they influence personal community relationships. Religious socialization is important not only because it provides the individual with a world view, but because it channels, individuals into personal communities that sustain a particular world view through the adult years.

Aleaz (2002) discussion on the typical characteristics of tribal religion under the title of 'nature-human-spirit continuum' includes the absence of written scripture, human made images or temples, oral tradition and natural objects as an accepted symbol of the divine. Halverson (1998) put forward the same view regarding the features of animism on the perspective of life is totally different from the Western non-religious view of life therefore he listed out the key elements to reach tribal peoples in which missionaries to be aware of to place the Church of the Supreme God among them. Anwals, a very superstitious people were studied by Bisht (2001) views that Anwals are Hindus by religion, are in the stage of polytheism according to the 'law of three stages'. The socio - cultural, economic and religious life controlled and regulated by the force of the respective supernatural being and they are celebrating Hindu religious festivals at the global as well as local level with certain variations.

Sharma (2011) discussion about the rich tradition of religion and culture of the tribal communities of Assam, which are based on supernaturalism, reveals that there are 30 plants belonging to 23 families are used for magico religious beliefs in Dobur Uie of Mising. It is noted that the use of plants in Dobur Uie ritual in need of urgent conservation, as their elimination may peril the rich tradition of Mising. Pathania (2008) study among the adolescents of Kinnaur, Lahaul-Spiti and Chamba districts of Himachal Pradesh indicated that almost all of them still had faith in supernatural powers and most of them observe religious activities daily in the form of prayer and the remaining performed it sometimes. Prayer, divination, ritual, festivals and the changes in their observances are discussed by Choudhary (2004). In the contemporary religious life of Konds all the deities are not worshipped in traditional fashion and the duration of trance also reduced and they practice the festivals of Hindus such as Deepavali, Rathyatrhra etc. Today the younger generation seems to be having dualistic religious approach as the conversion to Christianity is occurring due to the benefits of school education and hospital facilities.

Ancestor worship among the Lo Dagace of West Africa explained Goody (1962) to show that the belief of the father had eternal rights to the property as he held when he alive will reduce the subconscious desire for the death of his father for possession of the property which prevented till the father's death. Therefore the rituals and practices reveal some socio, psychological reflections. The same we can see in the ritual of *pambinthullal* the possession ritual in Kerala. She is a microcosm of the relationship between the members of the *tharavadu* and powers that can threaten to destroy its well being. Therefore the destruction of the *kalam* is a symbolic act that celebrates the restoration of this cosmic order through the enclosement of disorder in ritual. The symbolic interpretation of purity and pollution is discussed by Douglas (1964) to explain the more the social system put forth strain on the person involved in it, and it reflects the rituals of purity and impurity figure a unity in experience and contributed positively by means of penance that were positively publicly displayed and these symbolic patterns, disparate elements were related and disports experience was given meaning. Chihamba rituals also represent symbolic actions as discussed by Turner (1961) which show the relationship between social processes and symbolic action. The Chihamba ritual system of Africa encloses illustrative models of the cosmos and the place as society within it, using metaphors drawn from relatives between persons rather than from the relationship between things as the western person. But there are cases of sacred specialists which were both tribal and Hindu castes resides in a village is discussed by Mishra (2004). To him there are four types of sacred specialist such as 1) Pahan is the sacred specialists of the tribes, who, assisted by pujar in the sacred performances and selection of the Pahan is hereditary. Second one is the Brahmin and his assistants are indispensable for most of the sacred performances made by Hindus in general and tribal in particular. Third one is the different hinduised bagats such as kamaru bagat, mali bagat, nagamati bagat, Nemha bagat. He is discussing the different roles playing these specialists in the village.

The significance of supernaturalism in the livelihood of tribal people is observed by Vidhyarthi (1963). The nature, man and spirit interaction in the daily life of tribal people is explained as; under the heading nature explores the ecological settings of the matter. Under the heading man, describes the social institutions such as marriage, family and under the heading spirit deals with the spirit and the supernatural world.

A dangerous trend, which question the identity of human beings occur with the changes in the religious life of human beings. Pohlong (2004) argues that culture and religion are ways of life where each one is inclusively related to each other and when the religion removed from the culture it merely a blind faith in God, and fanatic attachment with a set of rituals, beliefs, practices, priest, craft, etc. Therefore the religion is an extremely powerful motivation of behavior forms basis for social and cultural identity any changes in religious identity corroborate to the loss of cultural identity. The social customs, manners and its transformation both structural and functional part is discussed by Singh (2000) with the illustration of the rituals, norms and practices have moderately intimate connection with the religious beliefs and practices of every tribe and has their own unique features in celebration of the festivals. It is also noted that the impact of social customs and religious factors keeping the tribal economy at low productivity stage has been found astounding.

Social phenomena and religion as an integral part of the social structure of the community has analyst by Troisi (2000) with the role of religion in Santhal social life and its interaction is crucial as all spirits are malevolent and enemies of man. The seasonal rituals and festivals and the actual relationship between magic manifest the santhal's dependence on religion. Moreover the religious changes occurred due to the interaction with the Hinduism and Christianity. Cases of religious conversion in Africa observed by Comaroff (1991) views it as merely a part of a larger socio-cultural and ideological changes taking place among the people, therefore the conversion offers only a limited contribution hence it has no significance as such it is simply catalyst in a wider socio- historical movement. The changes undertook from tradition to modernity among the Todas with the course of time has noted by Walker (1998) and discuss about the pollution huts are eliminate by the Toda caste council because it is unease during cold and monsoon months, even though the rituals are still performing with certain variation upto the changing time like ear piercing ceremony, which has been shifted from Toda hamlets to Hindu temples and new generation seems to be in full acceptance of the two parallel ritual systems of their own as well as Hinduism. The socio, cultural and political circumstances with regard to Hindu objections to conversion are deep-rooted in the religious philosophy and traditions. That have been discussed by Kim (2003) with the Indian theology and missionaries to the Hindus objections will reveal that Christian emphasis on human rights and of the Hindu tradition of tolerance will be crucial for the future of Hindu Christian relations in India.

Traditional religion of the people of Arunachal Pradesh identified by Dawar's (2003) as Bodic, who are following Buddhism and Non Bodic group, who are following the tribal religion based on nature worship. Adi tribe, a Non Bodic group experiences the Christianization and by defending its cultural practices and also reforming some aspects of culture the elite counter with the Christianization.

Therefore the above reviews observes the existence of a common moral order or system of values which binds people together in community as an explanation of social interaction under the umbrella of religion. These normative systems, rituals, and common practices are treated as the central fabric of social relations; they are thus an essential feature of the community. Religion signifies the inner experience which reveals to the mind the real meaning and purpose of life, it is the very soul of culture. This great variation in the cultures with the changes in religion shows the social changes occurs along with the religious mobility. When it is used for external form in which the inner experience has crystallized itself, it is only a part of it. From these observations and explanations the present study formulates its hypothesis and objectives.

Hypothesis

- Contact with outsiders may cause the changes in socio religious aspects.
- Economic reasons may cause religious conversion.
- Mass media may influence the changing world view of the people.

Objectives

The focus of the present study is to document the religious life of Thachanadan Moopan of wayanad district in Kerala. The close contact with alien culture of mainstream people influenced them and it is visibly seen in the socio cultural life of the Thachanadan Moopan.

> **To document the belief system and supernaturalism of Thachanadan Moopan.**
> **To evaluate the changes occured in the religious life of the Thachanadan Moopan.**

Methodology

The data for the present study collected through the anthropological methods and techniques. Survey method conducted to get censes report of the particular study. The survey was conducted by canvassing a schedule to get data on, house type, water sources, security arrangements, electricity, occupation etc accompanied by informal interviews.

Observation method is useful to document various types of rituals and performances. Participant observation is suitable to some areas and non-participant observation is suitable to some areas. In most of the cases participant and non-participant observation is accompanied with formal or informal interviews. Those available details are cross checked with 3 or 4 respondents again. Case study method is more suitable to understand the cause and consequence of religious conversion. In addition to this secondary data was gathered from official sources. Tape recorder was used to record some songs, which used to praise their god and goddess. Photo albums pertaining to different occasions in the life of the Thachanadan moopan, available with different families, have also been used to identify and understand various rituals and marriage ceremonies.

Limitations of the study

Religion is an area, which is most sensitive and closer to the life of the people. Therefore strong rapport establishment is essential if reliable and in-depth data is to be collected. Their rigid customs and manners also posed a difficulty in obtaining their inner meaning. Nevertheless, by cross checking with different informants, efforts had been made to keep such gaps to the minimum.

Selection of the field

The field for the present study is in the Wayanad district of Kerala. Wayanad is the holyland of the tribal people of Kerala. The area accounts for 29 percent of the total population of the Kerala. Kurichians, Mullukurumbas, Uralikurumbas, Paniyans, Adiyans and Kattunaikkans are the main Scheduled Tribe communities inhabiting Wayanad. But there are other communities like Thachanadan Moopan, Wayanadan Kadarm Wayanad pulayans, Kunduvadiyans who are not included in the Scheduled Tribe list even though most of them exibit tribal characteristics (Ramanunni 2002: 67). As the study is about the tribe, Thachanadan Moopan were selected for the purpose. Thachanadan Moopan is mainly concentrated in the areas such as Mepadi, Kalpatta and sulthan bathery. The selected settlements for the present study were kadachikunnu, kottanad, kallumal, chengollam were pilot surveyed. The settlements of Thachanadan Moopan are scattwered. This is mainly because of their retreat in to the forest areas. Thus some of the settlements are in thecforest areas with out much contact with outsiders and other settlements are with cnon tribal groups.

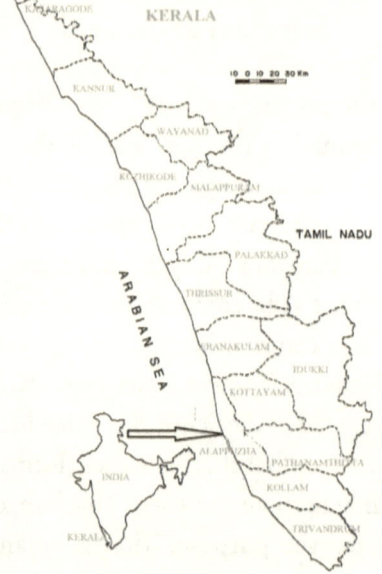

Map: Kerala State

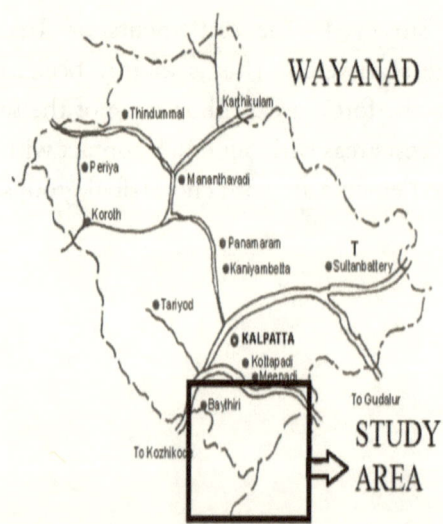

Map: Wayanad District

From the previous study about the Thachanadan Moopan as part of the P.G course knowledge acquired about the field situations. The present study is mainly concentrated on the settelements of kadachikkunnu, Kottanadu, Kallumala and cheengollam. The selection of these areas is mainly because of the transportation problem and time. As the field work is time bound objectified to the duration of the course not possible to go interior areas. As the research topic is related to religion data should not get only through the interview methods. But the researcher should have close interaction with respondents. Thus the area for the present study is mainly concentrated in four settlements.

2

BELIEF SYSTEMS AND
SUPERNATURALISM OF
THACHANADAN MOOPAN

Religion designates an individual's interaction to the supernatural power and the various organised systems of beliefs and customs on those supernatural powers are worshipped. Occurrence of unexpected dilemma like disease, death and other incidents like flood, draught, thunder etc. made the early man to believe in the supernatural power. Therefore religion represents the idea of propitiation of these supernatural powers for the goodness of mankind. This provides us an image of supernatural power, which is strange, mysterious and enigmatic in nature and worshipped in the form deities, gods and goddesses, ghosts and souls. Debashish (2003) classification of supernatural among the indigenous of India as supreme deity, village tutelary deities, sub clan spirits, household spirits, ancestral spirits, malevolent or evil spirits and regional Hindu deities which are borrowed to the tribal religious pantheon. At the same Vidhyarthi (1983) classified tribal religion and practices under different headings such as sacred objects, sacred beliefs, sacred pantheons, and sacred specialists and sacred centres. The concept of sacred and profane was introduced Durkhiem () with the notion of human identify day to day issues or incidents as profane (outside the temple) and the incidents of inspirational or admiration as sacred. Inshort distinguishing sacred and profane acts of life is the essence of religious belief. Therefore the present chapter is to deal with the supernaturalism of Thachanadan Moopan, within the frame work of sacred complex which includes the sacred objects, beliefs, pantheon, specialists, centres, performances etc.

Sacred Objects

Sacred objects in religion is always in association with myth or legend related to the object which is considered as sacred in religion. For example, the *Rudraksha* to a Hindu, Bible or a Cross for the Christian and Quran for Muslim. The sacred objects include all things that are considered worthful to worship and with reverence to a particular area. These sacred objects are worshipped and propitiated through ritualistic performance with the belief that the deity resides in. Thus the sacred objects which are worshipped by the members of the Thachanadan Moopan identified many sacred things in the settlements of Thachanadan Moopan and they state that, each sacred object is important for certain purpose.

Kanayam

Kanayam consists, a bunch of sticks. *Kanayam* is made out of branches from Jack fruit (*Artocarpus heterophyllus*) tree. It is dangled in the corner of the room along with peacock feathers, usually the *kanayam* is kept on the deer horn and that is tied in the roof. The room, where the *kanayam* is kept, is known as *karanavastanam*. Thachanadan Moopan believes that *kanayam* is the object in which the ancestral spirits (*chali muthachi*) resides. *Kanayam* is the most important object of *kulam* (lineage) and *tharavadu* (clan) of Thachanadan Moopan. *Kanayam*, is also the symbol of authority, only found in *moopan*, *lepan*, and *chali thekkanam*'s house. So it is not available or no one can have it in one's own house. In a few cases a single individual may hold all these three positions. The absence of male members in the *tharavadu* leads to the extinction of that *tharavadu,* likewise the absence of women in the *chaali* lead the *chaali* in to extinction. Thus in such cases if a person is the *moopan* of a *tharavadu*, and in his *chaali* no other male members are there to take care the position he can take both *moopan* and *theakkanam* (head of the *chaali*) position. Another case if the person who has the *kanayam* of *moopan* or *lepan* or *theakkanam* is hinduised or christianised and he is not at all interested to continue the position another person can take the position. In such case, the *kanayam* of the respective positions kept in different and in respective places of his house. Because now a day some of the *tharavadu*s and *chali*s are in the stage of extinction due to the shortage of people. As the title is hereditary, the objects are handed over from generation to generation. *Kanayam* of *tharavadu* is transfered hereditarily, but *kanayam* of *chali* is passed on elderly basis. The member of a *tharavadu* can not touch the *kanayam* However the member of the particular *tharavadu* can touch their *kanayam. Tharavadu kanayam,* the residence of *kurikal* (the male ancestral spirits) can not be taken outside the boundary of that *tharavadu,* and *chali kanayam* is shifted to the place of the *chali thekkanam* as the position is held on the elderly basis, and there is no restriction in the movement of *chali kanayam.*

Bimbam (Stone)

The representations of deities are done by Thachanadan Moopan using stone. Instead of idols they utilize stones. Usually they use stones of triangular form, as they believe that, it represents or symbolizes the mountain, their dwelling place. The stones representing their deities are placed in mud platforms, which are called as *mandapam.*

Val (sword) and Pattu (A piece of cloth)

Thachanadan Moopan are worshipping the objects, which are considered as the weapons of their gods and deities. *Bagavathi* is the goddess of Thachanadan Moopan. They believe, *val* (Sword) is the weapon of *bagavathi.* The sword is made out of iron and brass. Hence they observe it as a sacred object. It is not allowed to be kept either in the house or in the sacred groves; it is kept in a separate hut with in the settlement. It is also permissible to keep it in the temple only during *uthsavam* (festivals) times. While getting the possession of *bagavathi* they use the weapon to symbolize that he or she is possessed by *bagavathi*. *Pattu*, a red coloured cloth, is also considered as the clothing of *bagavathi*. It is also kept in the separate hut along with *val*. This is used during the time of *velichapadu* (oracle).

Mayilpeeli (Feather of Peacock)

There is a myth about the *mayilpeeli* (peacock feather) is as follows, Thachandan Moopan believe that *karivilli kariyathan* came to the forest as *malankuravan* and *malankurathi*. To help them there were *muthan* and *muthi* (refers old male and female). They had seven sons and six daughters. Later this *muthan* died. *Muthi* went to another *kunnu* (hill) and their children also followed. The people believe that the *muthi* and the 13 children are not dead instead disappeared. During the period of disappearance, peacocks came there and drop out feathers as a symbol of blessing. These seven sons became seven *kurikkals* and six daughters with *muthi* became *chalumuthachi*. Peacock feather is also considered as a sacred object and is kept along with *kanayam*. It is related to their ancestral worship.

Ponthi (Iron rod)

Ponthi, is a short iron rod, is believed as, the weapon of the deity *gulikan*. It is kept in the house of the *karanavar*. It is used only during the time of festivals.

Sacred Beliefs

Every society has certain beliefs and practices and in the case of indigenous groups these belief in supernatural is stiff in nature. A person, who is convinced of the truth of a statement is said to have a belief (Nair 2008:138). Sacred beliefs of indigenous groups are those beliefs and myths that are related to the religious life of an individual. Different types of beliefs and faiths existing among tribes in the form of myths, legends, folk tales, folk songs etc.

Myth

The tribal people have their own myths related to the clan, the place, the village etc. and these myths or legends explain the origin or the development of the same and direct the people to worship and perform the rituals to propitiate the deity or spirit in their myths. These myths are preserved and transmitted orally from one generation to another. They observe certain folk dances and folksongs which praise the charactors in myths in accordance to the preservation. The myth explains a ceremony or character in its structural and functional part. There may be a romantic or heroic story of some historical person or figure which may finally gives the tribal group their clan or family god. Therefore the unnatural occurances are treated as the displeasure of these mythical charactors who are not worshipped appropriately. Briefly the fear of spirits or mythical charactors results in human actions is for the rightiousness of the humanworld.

Myth about the Origin

There is a popular myth associated with origin of name of the community as how the people recollect it. Choondal (2003) says that there was a conflict between *eleri* and *mothali* in Nilamboor and at last *eleri* beaten (*thachu) mothali*. As *mothali* is superior in position, by fear of punishment *eleri* with his family and relatives escaped to Wayanad. *Elery* and *mothali* are the equivalent terms for *moopan* and *lepan* in Wayanad. In Thachanadan Moopan dialect beaten refers *thachu*. It is belived by the people thus they got the name Thachanadan.

There are several myths regarding the origin of Thachanadan Moopan. According to one, there was a war between *Maruveed Nairs* and *Pattars* (two different caste groups in Kerala) of Nilambur. In this war *Maruveed Nairs* defeated. After the war there is only one baby in *pattar* family alive. All the men died and females escaped from that area. The *Pattar* decided to take him to Nilambur and decided to look after him. He is grown up and became a young energetic person. He fell in love with a girl of Maruveed Nair family named Meenakshiamma. He brought her from Nilambur Kovilakam to his native land. As per the custom *marumakkathayam,* (*Marumakkathayam* was an ancient custom followed by some Nair families (a faction of Hindus) of Kerala. According to this, the property rights of the joint family were vested with female members. A man's children had no rights in the family as they belonged to the wife's family) the *karanavar* (head of the family) partitioned her properties. Thus, meenakshiamma get the properties in Chembra Peak. To help Meenakshiamma and her husband one *koodan* and *koodathi* (servants belonging to lower caste) accompanied them. Thachanadan Moopan believes that they are the followers of this *koodan* and *koodathi*. In Nilambur, they have known as *malankoodar*. As these people reside in *mala* means hill. When they came to wayanad their neighbours called them *wayanadan koodar*. Therefore Thachanadan Moopan also known as *Wayanadan koodar*.

Etymology of Thachanadan Moopan

The name is reported to have originated from their place of origin *Thachanad*. (Maralusiddhiah 2002: 1381). The place Thachanad is situated in their place Nilambur. This is in Malappuram district of Kerala. It is situated close to the Nilgiris range of the Western Ghats on the banks of the Chaliyar river. These people narrate the legend about the suffix *moopan* in the community name as Thachanadan Moopan. There are so many tribes in Wayanad area such as Thachanadan, Paniyan, and Kattunaickan etc., when landlord of that area decided to give the position of *Moopan* (Moopan means head) to each and every group all the *adivasis* (tribes) went. But the *Thachanadan* was not present there. Thus the landlord told them to take the position of *Moopan* to all of the Thachanadans. Thus, they get the suffix *moopan* from the ruler *kottayathu Thamburan* of Kanthamangalam fort at Kottapadi in Vythiri thaluk (Choondal 2003:43)

Myth about Kanayam

Kanayam (consists of wooden sticks) is a symbol of authority. The *kanayam*, which represents the position of *moopan, lepan* and *chali thekkanam*. Thus it is found in the house of *moopan*'s *lepan*'s and *chali thekkanam*'s. It kept in the room called *karanavasthanam*. Their main deity is *karivilli kariyathan*. The myth about *kanayam* revolves around the stories of *karivilli kariyathan*. They believe that *karivilli kariyathan* is incarnation of Lord Shiva and Parvathi in one figure. Once they appeared as *malankuravan* and *malankurathi* in the jungle. The ancestors of Thachanadan Moopan helped them by clearing the forest. *Karivilli kariyathan* had a stick in their hand which is used to clear the forest. *Karivilly kariyathan* gave that stick to *muthan, muthi* and their children those who lived in the forest for the survival in the wild forest. Thachanadan Moopan believed that *muthan muthi* and their children didn't died still live in this sticks. Thus they worship *kanayam,* the wooden sticks. Over generations they are used to hand over from one to other. They are making coral marks on those sticks (*kanayam*) to identify the number of generations used that. The coral marks are done after the performance of *adiyanthiram*. After the death of the *moopan* of a *tharavadu* or *chali* on the thirtieth day they are performing the *adiyanthiram. Adiyanthiram* is the ceremony conducted after thirty-three days from the day of death. By performing *adiyanthiram,* they believe that the dead person's soul would go to the group of ancestors. Otherwise they may roam in the earth as ghosts. After that function the *moopan*s of the 35 *tharavadu*s take that *kanayam* and clean it with river water. Then who ever get possessed that time takes it and makes a coral on it on the right side of the *kanayam*. Then they take the *kanayam* to the *karanavasstanam* a cleaned mortar kept facing downward. Then the selection of the new *karanavar* is done and takes the *kanayam* in to his house. But in case of *lepan* there is no selection function rather they directly take the *kanayam* in to the new *lepan*'s house because the selection is based on age.

Once in a year *kanayam* brought to *kurikkal mandapam* and they perform *pooja* and return to their home and perform *vechoottu karmam*. It is also known as *panthrandu oottu*. They use raw rice to prepare food and with plantain leaves they prepare *padam* and the prepared food kept inside *padam* and placed in front of *kanayam*. This ceremony is done by *tharavadu karanavar*. Women are not permitted to do or to take part in this ceremony. At the end part of the ceremony the performer roll back five or seven lines of silver thread around *kanayam*

The myth about mayilpeeli and ancestral spirits

The myth about *mayilpeeli* (peacock feather) is as related to earlier myth follows. The *muthan* and *muthi* who helped *karivilli kariyathan* when came to the forest as *malankuravan* and *malankurathi*. The people believe that the *muthi* and the 13 children they are not died but disappeared. During the period of disappearance, peacocks comes there and drop out feathers. Thachanadan Moopans believe that while disappearing *muthachi*'s and *kurikkal*'s give their blessings through the peacock feather. Thus they keep *mayilpeeli* (peacock feather) near *kaanayam*. *Muthan* is also called as *muthappan*. Based on the *muthachi* they divided *chaali*. Each *chaali* based on female ancestor spirit called *muthachi*. Some *chali's* are considering sister *chalis* also. Like that each *kunnu* or *tharavadu* is classified under each *kurikkal*. Therefore Thachanadan Moopan are the followers of the ancestral spirits *kurikkal* and *muthachi*. Both *tharavadu* and *chali* are exogamous in nature. An individual's *tharavadu* is from his/her father and *chali* is from his/her mother. Thus, each and every one has their own *tharavadu* and *chali*, they should not marry with in the *chali* or *tharavadu*.

Taboos

The term taboo in cultural studies describe any prohibition resting in the day to day life. Taboo occupies a very important position in the religious life of the Thachanadan Moopan. There is a taboo about the *kanayam* that nobody out side the *tharavadu* and *chali* is permitted to touch *kanayam* and marriage between the members of *tharavadu* and *chaali* is also prohibited. If a person of one *tharavadu* and *chali* died the taboo known as *pula* goes on the members of that *tharavadu* and *chaali* members only. *Pula* is observed for thirty days. From the day of death to three days the dead person's wife has to sitting in a hut called *balipera* and her hair is let loosened. She is not allowed to enter in to the house. His *tharavadu* and *chaali* people will not take non vegetarian food till thirtieth day. They can not practice or participate in any sacred performances. They do not go to temples also. For the first three days they do not prepare food in the dead person's house. In case of a person's wife is dead, and then he should not do the performance of cutting hair and shaving beard for a period of 30 days.

Women are prohibited to enter the house for the first four days when they were in menstruation period. They remained isolated in a hut which was constructed temporarily. They are also prohibited to cook food in these days. They are not allowed to go to temples/ *kaavu* /the room consisting *karanavastanam*. In earlier period during puberty period the girl was not allowed to come in front of the males for four days. Even a women in her period has to sleep with out her husband. The pregnant woman is not allowed to go to temples / *kaavu* / the room consisting *karanavastanam* from the seventh month of pregnancy to three months after delivery. After delivery the mother and new born child were secluded in a room for a period of four days and the mother has to maintain pure and separate diet. It is believed that if these taboos are not obeyed properly the child may face diseases and evil spirits may attack them. Consumption of buffalo or cow meat, snake and peacock as food is prohibited by the Thachanadan Moopan. Nursing mother or feeding mother should not eat jackfruit. Consumption of the fruits such as Papaya, pineapple, sugar cane, is prohibited to pregnant women up to her 6th or 7th months.

Omens

Even in day to day lives Thachanadan Moopan observe some supernatural influences. By this they say the coming actions or incidents may good or bad. Many people all over the world have held fast to the belief in omens and auspicious moments (Crooke 1925: 12). Thachanadan Moopan believes that by seeing these omens they can escape from the unlucky events.

- They believe that crowing of a crow in the courtyard fore tells the coming of the guest in the house.
- They believed this may be they may prepare more food items to provide the invited guests and there is too much waste is there compared to other days. Thus the crows may come and make noise. Whenever crow is there those people say guest is expected.
- If a person wakes up and if she or he happens to see mirror, or a pot full of water or lamp is considered to be lucky for that person.
- Psychologically by see is a pot full of water in the morning itself one may get pleasure to the mind and then get energetic.
- Mirror should not be shown to babies because the mirror reflect sunlight in the day time this may harm the eyes of the child while in the night time by seeing other things in the mirror child may get frightened.
- It is a bad omen, especially for a person who is just leaving for a purpose, if he sees a widow, with an empty earthen pot.

Evil Eye

It is believed that some human beings and animals cast on evil eye (Chettiar 2002: 45). Thachanadan Moopan has belief in evil eye, i.e. those who possess an evil eye have the power to influence the object by simply looking it. In the opinion of Thachanadan Moopan the evil eye and bad omens may also cause diseases and misfortune. The man or woman who possesses these eyes can bring ruin to a person, destroy his household members, domestic animals, crops and houses. They said that evil eye mostly affecting the person, who have lot of wealth, beautiful and healthy children, pregnant women etc. If the evil eye falls on the wealth of a person his harvest may be destroyed, if it affects the health of a child it may suffer from diseases, if it is on a pregnant women delivery may become too difficult.

Sacred Pantheon

The concept sacred pantheon refers to the Gods, Godesses, spirits or deities of a community that they worship. It is also noted that these gods, deities or spirits are there for the well being of the community and worshipped by them. The concept of relationship of the spiritual beings with the doings of man involves the idea of supernatural power, and this idea has given rise to the notion of fate which means the power of an impersonal force (Kattakayam 1983:145).

Karivilli kariyathan

The supreme deity of the Thachanadan Moopan is *karivilli kariyathan*. The myth about the origin of Thachanadan Moopan community, which has been described earlier related to this deity. They believe that *karivilli kariyathan* came to the forest as *malankuravan* and *malankurathi* (hunters). To assist them in the forest there is a *muthan* and *muthi*. This *muthan* and *muthi* and their children are the ancestors of the Thachanadan Moopan. They believe that *karivilli kariyathan* still alive in the hill called Velloor *mala*. Thus, nobody is allowed to go there. Once the *karivilli kariyathan* came as oracle and give the order that, "I have 18 *katakam* (Aboard of *karivilly Kariyathan*) in different parts of the forest you should keep clean at these places. Among the 18 *katakam* (The term *katakam* refers to aboard of deity) 7 are important, namely, 1) Thenevaram, 2) Valathur 3) Peraty, 4) Perumthattu, 5) Payamuty, 6) Kottuthara, 7) Pathilambalam. Other important worshipping centeres or sacred groves are in Kadachikkunnu, Kottanad, Chembothara, Cheengollam, Ambalavayal, Kadooru, Pulloorpadi, Puttyad. The term *katakam* refers to aboard of deity.

Among these seven places different forms of *kariyathan* exists. These seven forms are called *ezhappanmar*. From this *7 kadakam, 18 kadakam* derived. To assist *kariyathan* there are seven members called *ezhuvillanmar* (seven watchers). They are the watchman's (*kavalkar*) of *karivilli kariyathan*. They believe that *karivilli kariyathan* is the owner of the entire land. In any *pooja* or any ceremony the first position should be given to *karivilli kariyathan*.

Gulikan

Gulikan is one of the deities of Thachanadan Moopan. *Gulikan* exists in different names as *agni gulikan, chemmakuluvan, chora gulikan. Gulikan* always possess with weapon called *ponthi.* This is a short iron rod. *Gulikan* is considered as the *kavalkaran* (watcher) of the *kunnu* (hill). The idol of *gulikan* is in the *moopan's* house and in *kaavu* (sacred grove) too. Before each and every hunt, the people go and seek permission of the *gulikan* and also they worship it for a good hunt too. At this point, some one possess oracle of *gulikan*, usually by *moopan* or *lepan*, but not necessarily, and any one can have the possession. In the action, the *velichapadu* (the person who possess the oracle) query the gathering, "what you will give to me?" the gathering will reply as "we offer you the liver of the hunted animal" and the gathering humbly request the *gulikan* that, "whether it should be roasted or not?" If the *velichapadu* says, raw then the hunted animal is shared among the group of hunters and the liver is taken and offered in front of the idol situated in *kaavu,* If the *velichapadu*, asking for the roasted one, then they bring hunted game to the settlement and then they take off the liver from the game and the *moopan* fry the liver and offer it front of the idol of *gulikan*, placed under the Banyan tree. After that the meat cut and giving to whomever gathered there. There are some sacred performances related with *gulikan* especially *narukku vekkuka* ceremony.

NaruckuVekkuka

This ceremony is performed for *gulikan*. This ceremony is performing according to ones wish. When one person facing any problem or to say thanks to the god for some purposes etc. They take a plantain leaf and cut it into 21 or 41 pieces of equal sizes and placed them in the platform in a round shape. It is known as *naruku*. A circle is drawn by using a kind of powder, which is prepared of rice. *Malar* (popped rice) and rice are also put beside it. Then equal numbers of threads are fixed on the *naruku*. There are two types of *thiri* (thread) namely *patuthiri and mukkanam thiri*. The *mukkanam thiri* has three branches but the *patuthiri* had only one branch. For the *narukku vekkuka* ceremony they are using only *patuthiri*. Inside the 21 or 41 *naruk* (pieces of plantains leaf), they arrange plantains leaf in a circular form and fill them with turmeric water or water made out of *kari* (charcoal). Then the *moopan* prays in front of it to rend the blessings from god.

Bhagavathi

Bagvathi is the Goddess of Thachanadan Moopan. *Bagavathi* also exists in different forms and names such as *cheriya bagavathi, valiya bagavathi, choorukundu bagavathi* etc. *Bagavathi* is also called *thamburaty*. Sword is the weapon of *bagavathi* and *pattu* is the cloth of *Bagavathi*.

Mariamman

Mariamman is considered as the goddess of health. It is believed that the diseases like smallpox and chikken poxes are easily cured by visiting and praying *mariamman*.

Ancestral spirits

Ancestral worship is supposed to have developed out of the cult of the dead and the propitiation of ghosts particularly

the propitiation of the diseased members of the family
(Nair 2008: 49). There is a myth about ancestral spirits of
Thachanadan Moopan. It is believed that ancestors are the
helpers of *karivilli kariyathan*. Thachanadan Moopan are
the descendents of these ancestral spirits. As per the myth,
muthan and *muthi* have six daughters and seven sons. The
muthi and six daughters form the seven *muthachi* of 101
chali (lineage) and the seven sons are the *kurikkal* of 36
padi (clan). Based on this *muthachi* and *kurikkal,* the *padi*
and *chali* divisions have been formed. They have the belief
that the head part of the *muthan* has been severed in a
war and he became two half *kurikkals* and become a stone.
Thus, he has come to be known as *aravayavan* who is also
called *muthappan*. He has the supreme position among the
ancestral spirits.

Chali Muthachi (Ancestral spirit of Chaali)

Chali muthachi is the ancestral spirit of the *chaali* (lineage).
Totaly there are seven *chali muthachi*s. Few *chaali*'s forms
the sister *chaali*' hence each *chali muthachi* is the ancestral
spirit of a group of sister *chali's*.

1. *makki muthachi*
2. *vellathi muthachi*
3. *kallyani muthachi*
4. *kunthi muthachi*
5. *nellumuth muthachi*
6. *karippi muthachi*
7. *naranichi muthachi*

In the case of *chaali*'s womens are giving importance. As they are performing *chaali* exogamy, the marriage with in the *chaali* is prohibited. As sister *chaali*'s are there the marriage between these *chaali*'s also prohibited. The sister *chaali*'s are the follows;

Table 2.1: Sister *chali's*

Edoor Chali (8 *Chali*)	Naalu Chali (4 *Chali*)	Munoor Chali (3 *Chali*)	Randu Chali (2 *Chali*)
Pommaramer	Madamer	Manjalammer	Kattumpanthi
Lerkumaer	Mattupanthi	Merkkanmaer	Kandrukkar
Miriyakka-panthi	Mundamer	Melu thakk-kanmaer	-
Kolkampanthi	Chenna maer	-	-
Pathrakam-panthi	-	-	-
Mavumare	-	-	-
Kottaikkar	-	-	-
Mangadamau	-	-	-

Kurikkal (Ancestral spirit of Tharavadu)

Kurikkal is the ancestral spirits of the *tharavadu* (clan). Each *tharavadu* had it's own *kurikkal*. Some of the *tharavadus* are sister *tharavadus*. Thus they are coming under same ancestral spirit (*kurikkal*). The name of the ancestral spirit of the *tharavadu* and which *tharavadu*'s fall under the same ancestor are as follows.

Table 2.2: *Tharavadu* based on ancestral spirits (*Kurikkal*)

Pekkallu Kurikkal	Kallicheri kurikkal	Koleri kurikkal	Malankara kurikkal	Ilukkachery Kurikkal*	Chemmanichal muthappan**
Perunthattu	Kuruncheru	Chorameru	Kandrikkaru	Malameru	Pichattu karu
Kunnumbatta-karu	Pengirikaru	Karikarameru	Velakarameru	Miriyameru	Cheenaputhi
Poyamudy	Methiri katu	Changarameru	Kotakaru	Kannamkudam-meru	Choorumeru
Venguppally	Neruncheru	Malinjameru	Malankarakaru	Pulloorkunnu	Kantameru
Extincted	Muttil Karu	Karameru	Kappilkaru	Nechirimeru	Katamuttakaru
Extincted		Moothrameru	1 padi extincted	--	Olkatakaru
--	--	--	--	--	Maltumeru
--	--	--	--	--	Melthattukar

(*Tharavadu's* under this *kurikkal* generally known *asmuthachi moonnuthara*)*
(*Tharavadu's* under this *kurikkal* generally called *eyaranadu*)**

Magic

The word magic is defined as an institution that was private and secret that comprised three elements; A magician who performed magical action, magical rites, themselves and magical representations, which described the beliefs, ideas, surrounding ritual action (Nair 2008). Magic is found in the supernatural world of Thachanadan Moopan. Their magic is known us *odiyan pani* or *odi vekkuka*. Thachanadan Moopan practice sorcery and witchcraft. They practice these mainly to cure the diseases. In olden times diseases were lesser compared to present time. Because during the past they used the food items from the forest. That is fresh and good. But now they are using modern food available in the shop. That was one of the main reasons for the disease among the tribal people. They had remedies to cure the diseases. According to their belief system, herbal medicines and magical spells could cure diseases. The techniques on understanding about magic, and also techniques about ethno-medicine preserved by some specialists and it was not open to public. Knowledge in the magical practices is accessible only to a few selected persons among them and they could keep them as secret and treat them as most valuable treasure. This secret knowledge about medicinal plants and magical rites are always transferred orally through generations.

The person, who is doing these performances are generally called *chakran* or *chakrathi*. When a person falls ill, his or her relatives first try to apply the medicines they know. If this fails they call the *chakran* or *chakrathi to* cure the disease. To cure the diseases, they use magic. They believe that they have as much number of magic as the number of herbal medicines available to them.

Kandam vekuka or chaanam vekuka (Measuring)

Kandam vekuka is one of the magico-religious practices to find out the diseases. This is performed by *chakruthi* or *chakran,* by using manthras and they use herbal medicines to treat. *Chakruthi* or *chakran* measures the hand of the diseased person, from ankle to finger tip through the hand by spreading her hand thumb to point length. While measuring, they also chant manthras. If the measurement is not completed in the hand of the person, the person would not have any disease. If the measuring length is less than the hand, the disease must be serious. If the length ends in the palm, it is believed that it happens due to the dissatisfaction of the deity. They have a belief that vomiting and dysentery are caused by the dissatisfaction of the *bagavathi*. To cure the diseased person should propitiate the Goddess through the prayer. She/He also gives herbal medicines along with spelled water. It is believed that the disease will be cured.

They also believe that the person who collides with *karinkutty* (a deity) on his/her way, is afflicted with some mental disorder, and showing the symptoms such as eating soil or coal and scratching the fellow people. Magical practice is applied for curing this disease. Usually, a thread, which has seven knots, made after spelling mantras, is tied in the hand. It is believed that by tying thread on the hand they can kept away the evil spirits.

Magic is performed mainly to cure the disease like smallpox, measles, cold etc. They believe that smallpox is caused by wrath of the goddess *mariamma*. To propitiate the godess they offering *guruzi*. Even the herbal medicines can't prevent the disease they call the *velichapadu* (oracle). After getting in to trance he may say the disease may be because of the dissatisfaction of some gods or deities or somebody done witchcraft against that person or because of evil eye from a person.

Odiyanpani (Sorcery)

Their magic is locally called *odiyan pani* or *odi vekkuka*. In olden days it is strongly rooted in their day to day life. They are using *odiyan pani* to kill a person, destroy the harvest, to cause disease, to get a girl to marrie etc. Thus first they approch a magician and tell about his enemy or his problem to be solved. Then the magician writes the name and star along with *manthram* (mantras) on a copper plate. He buries it under the soil along the path expected to be taken by the enemy. If the enemy passes through the buried copper sheet, the person gets injured. If they want to destroy a farm, they bury the sheet in the field. Sometimes they are putting the chanted elements in to a pot and bury in the earth. If the pot is broken, i.e., by beating or kicking it is believed that will harms the performer. Another method they are using to kill a person is preparing a herbal poison out of some herbal and paste on the thorn *mullu murikku* (Mirabilis Jalapa) and keep on the way of his enemy. If the person touches it he will die with in seven days by vomiting blood. Thachanadan Moopan transferring all the knowledge related to black magic to nephew or son only, when he became a position to acquire such knowledge. But the lack of interest among new generation is a matter for the slow extinction of the knowledge from the society.

Mashinottam

In olden days, the *mashinottam* used to be very popular. This has always been used to find out the treasure and property. When any problem arises with regard to property, anything theft by anybody or anybody do against the wishes of deities or ancestors and so on, they resort to using this method to know who stolen the thing or the reason behind the problem. Those who know to do this continue to do it till now. To find out the reasons the performer, take a beetle leaf, and pasting a type of ink on it. This ink is made out of the eyes of *chemboth* (a bird) and *uppan* (a bird) are ground with some herbal medicines. After painting it in a beetle, palm or mixing it in water, they can see the things, which they want to find out. Where by the defaulter or the cause of the problem is detected.

Sacred Specialists

Sacred specialists refer to those people who are related to sacred things. The sacred rites and rituals are performed by these sacred specialists who have well knowledge and experience. They pass on their knowledge from generation to generation. All tribal groups have a priest or a group of sacred specialists, generally limited to two to three in number.

Moopan and Lepan

Moopan and *lepan* had multifarious works. *Moopan* is the head of the *tharavadu* and *lepan* is his assistant and deputy. Thus *moopan* and *lepan* have important role in the social, political and religious matters. *Moopan* performs all sorts of religious ceremonies; he led the important events of social and economic significance. And he acts as the doctor, who identifies the spirits responsible for causing diseases and prescribes the nature of sacrifices to be made. As a spiritual guide he secures blessing of the spirits by propitiating them time to time. In olden days people paid to him in the form of vegetables and ornaments. At present they pay in both cash and kind.

Moopan act as the priest of Thachanadan Moopan. In the past, when a child was born in the *tharavadu*, the mother must take the child in front of the *moopan* who would take the child infront of the *kanayam* to get the blessing of the ancestors. In the *kathukuthu kallyanam* (ear-boring ceremony), the ceremony was done in *moopan*'s house and the *kathukuthu (ear boring)* and naming were done by the *moopan*. The marriages were also conducted in the *moopan*'s house. *Moopan* fixed the marriage by saying 'I am fixing the marriage between us' (between the *moopan*s of two *tharavadu*). Thus the relation was between two *moopan*s. The *moopan* would handover the *panathali* to the groom and the groom tied it. The *moopan* also would ask *penpanam* (brideprice). During the death ceremony the *moopan* controlled the entire process and on the *adiyanthiram* he was responsible to answer the questions such as how the person died, do you give medicine properly raised by other *moopan*s.

The rituals celebrated in the temples would also be led by the *moopan*. The *moopan* used to take decisions by discussing with others. He also functioned as a medicine man. He had complete knowledge about his Community, about the rituals and about ethno medicines and the same had been passed on from generation after generation.

Velichapadu (Oracle)

Velichapadu has an important position in the ritual and related ceremonies of Thachanadan Moopan. *Velichapadu* acts as an intermediary or medium between God and ordinary people. The person who gets *darshanam* is the *velichapadu* on each occasion. *Darshanam* refers to the possession of the God, ancestral spirits or dead persons. Both male and female persons get *darshanam* (possession). After getting possession his/her body swings rhythmatically. Then he begins to answer the questions and offer solutions to difficulties and problems of the people who are gathered. All the persons, who is able to speak the matter thoroughly and clearly could beceome *velichapadu*. Seven or twenty one days of *noyamb* (fasting) is taken to become a *velichapadu*. If the ritual is small, the *noyamb* is for seven days. But to become a *velichapadu* on the occasion of *utsavam*, 21 days *noyamb* is a must. If they get the *darshanam* of god, the *velichapadu* wears white coloured clothes. While the *velichapadu* gets the *darshanam* of the goddess, they wear red cloth on the shoulder. For goddess, *velichapadu* wear *aramani* and has the Sword in hand. The *velichapadu* of Goddess calls the people as *makkalu* (Children) and the *velichapadu* of the god calls people *perakka* (children). Both mean same word children.

Velichapadu has role in several occasions, during *utsavam*, during the selection of *theackanam* of the *chali* (head of the *chali*), etc. If any problem is encountered in a family or *tharavadu,* they call the *velichapadu* to find out the reason. *Velichapadu* reveals the reason for the dissatisfaction of gods or goddess or ancestral spirits, the offence they have committed etc. and also gives orders and advices. When the *velichapadu* is called, the *tharavadu karanavar* gives new clothes to wear.

The *velichapadu* is also called during *adiyanthiram* to solve the problems related to death, during the selection of next *karanavar, etc.* When they go for hunting, *velichapadu* of *gulikan* is called and asked about the hunting.

In *utsavam,* each and every *thira* is associated with a *velichapadu.* For example, the *thira* of *karivilli kariyathan* is associated with the *velichapadu* of *karivilli kariyathan.* Similarly, *bagavathi* and *gulikan* also have *thira* and *velichapadu.* Each and every *tharavadu* has its own members to perform *velichapadu.* If there is no one to perform the role they take from other families by paying money.

Chakrathi /Chakran (Medicine Woman or Man)

All the old people especially those who have knowledge about medicine are called as *chakran* or *chakrathi* in the dialect of Thachanadan Moopan. They have curing ways to most of the diseases. Long years of experience made him an expert in such matters. There were only a few such people. They use herbal plants and *manthras* to cure diseases. If the disease is minor, they only give the charmed water. Sometime they give thread to wear in the body. They also have a practice of *kandam vekkal,* in which the *chakruthi* measures the hand of the patient, to determine the nature of disease.

Diseases and herbal treatment

It was customary that, when a person is affected by disease, children or women in the *tharavadu* inform about it to *tharavadu karanavar,* namely, *moopan* or *lepan.* He comes and enquires about it and gives appropriate guidance to call the expert people known as *chakarthi* or *chakran* to diagnose the problem.

Barrenness can be treated by taking a small banana and spell and blow it. On the fourth day of periods the barren lady should consume the banana.

After delivery, suckling mother may not have adequate milk for her child. They believe that it may be because of *gulikan* or other gods. They cure it by a spell or hymn for *gulikan* and tie the yarn or thread to the mother. Then the mother can give enough milk to the child.

Small pox: Neem was used for small pox and it is a good medicinal plant. They grind the leaves of neem and apply on the effected area. For small pox naikuruna or *vasoorivalli* is grind into a paste form and applies on the body.

Measles: For measles they use *toothavalli*. They use *naikuruna* and *vellavalli* for the treatment of measles.

Jaundice: For the treatment of jaundice, *keezharnelli,* cumin seed, and garlic are mixed with cow milk and drink it in empty stomach. Another preparation is for jaundice is that they grind *kasturi manjal* (curcuma aromatica) and mix it with fresh cow milk and drink in the empty stomach.

Fever: The symptom of fever is cured by *panichedi*.

Cold: Leaves of a herb locally known as *padavalli* in paste form is mixed with cow milk and apply on head. They prepare it home.

Head ache: They pluck the herb *vaathavalli* before sunrise and grind in it. But it should be applied on the middle of the head at the time of sunrise, and it should be continued for seven days. Apart from this, they use *alichatanvalli, kodinni,* for head ache. There are two kinds of *kodinni*, namely, *soorya kodinni* and *chandra kodinni*. Cane or rattan reed's buds grind on washing stone then it will look like sandal paste. It should be ground before sunrise and used for seven days.

Sacred geography

The tribals believe that they are fully surrounded by a number of gods and deities and super powers residing in all the places where their people are. So the whole tribal village and its vicinity may be treated as the sacred area of the tribal

gods and deities. After locating the sacred area, we come to
a single spot where many varieties of rituals and devotional
activities are carried on. These spots are called sacred centers
(Vidhyarthi and Rai 1976). Accordingly, the sacred area of
Thachanadan Moopan is the whole area of their habitation.
They believe that their supreme God *karivilli kariyathan* is
the owner of this sacred area.

Sacred centres

Sacred centers of Thachanadan are mainly sacred grove
(*kaavu), karanavastanam*, and the homestead. The sacred
area is believed as 12 *adi* (3 meter). There are no definite
demarcation symbols to show the sacred and profane areas.

Kaavu (Sacred Grove)

Sacred groves are small patches of forests conserved through
man's spiritual belief and faith (Dash 2005). *Kaavu* is the main
worship centre in which their main deity *karivillikariyathan*
stationed. It contains few trees, such as *kaatu chembakam*
(Michelia champaca), *pala* (Alstonia scholaris), *poomaram*
(Delonix regia), banyan tree, neem tree, *poola* (Bombax
ceiba) and other local wild trees are also found, that noone
is allowed to remove. If anybody violates this rule they will
be punished and as a consequence they are not allowed that
person to enter in to the *kaavu* any more because he has
dissatisfied the supernatural powers and deities. However by
giving offerings to the deities' one can propitiate the deities
and get pardoned. Which is conveyed through *velichapadu*

who come and say, allow him to enter in to the *kaavu*. It is here *(kaavu)* that they offer sacrifices to certain deities especially *bagavathi* and *gulikan* on festive occasions. The important rituals taking place in the *kaavu* is during the time of *uthsavam* (festival). It begins with the *pooja* to all gods, and then the oracle of every god and deity will come. *karpa pooja, kozhiyarakkal, kanalattam* are the rituals they perform in the *kaavu*.

Structure of the kaavu

In olden times, they believed that their god's *karivilli kariyathan*, *gulikan,* and *bagavathi* resided in their kaavu. Each god had their own *mandapam* (mud-platform), which is made up of a heap of soil, with a triangular shaped stone fixed. Now days they use stones and black stones to make *mandapam*. The *mandapam* is always constructed under a tree. The *kaavu* is always surrounded with a number of trees and bushes such as *kaatu chembakam* (Michelia champaca), *pala* (Alstonia scholaris), *poomaram* (Delonix regia), banyan tree, neem tree, *poola* (Bombax ceiba) and other local wild trees are also found. There are two places in the sacred grove called *uthmam* (pure place) and *adhamam* (impure). In *uthmam* there is no sacrifices but worshiping with the flowers. But in *adhamam* there are the sacrifices like *kozhiyarakkal* (Cutting the head of the hen to propitiate the deity). This *uthamam* place is beyond the 3 meters from the *kaavu*.

Kanalaattam (Firedance)

Kanalaattam is the ceremony in which, people are walking through the fire to propitiate the deity. This ceremony is done in the Malayalam month of *kumbham* and *meenam* (March and April). This performance is mainly performing in the temples like *mariyamman kovil* in Mepadi and *pathilambalam* in Kottanad. This ceremony is done at the time of annual celebrations. First, this function was started at *mariyamman kovil*. Afterwards, every temple started performing it. The persons doing this undergo fasting for 7 or 14 days, avoiding non-vegetarian food and sexual relations. On the day of *kanalattam,* they go to the river or stream for bath. After that, they perform *kanalaattam,* which means 'fire dance'. First they prepare a *kaavayi (*a long pit*)* with 2½ feet breadth and 20 feet length. Then, they put the coconut shell and wood of *poovam* (a tree). The wood is put in the *kavayi* in the shape of a roof. Then they make the kanal (fire) and the person's who offer to walk in this fastly walk through it. Before *kanalattam,* the people express their wishes and receive *basmam (ash)* from the *velichapadu* of *mariyamma.*

Kozhiyarakkal

The ritual *kozhiyarakkal* has to be performed at a place other than *uthamam* (pure*)* part of the sacred gove. This ritual is conducted during *utsavam* as a final part of the ceremony. In this ritual *moopan* first decides to enter into the *kurikkal mandapam.* In front of the *mandapam,* he offers coconut, beaten rice, and *malaru* (burst rice) in the plantain leaf to the *kurikkal*. Before giving the offer to the *bagavathi, kanayam* is struck in front of the *mandapam*. They fold the leaf before *kurikkal* and keep it. Then, they go to *bagavathi's mandapam*. There, they place before ancestralspirits the beaten rice, agarbathi, and cucumber. After bathing in the stream, the *moopan* return with the wet clothes and keep pot of water in his hand and spray the water using *karukkapullu* (Melanochelys trijuga coronata) on the way. He goes around the *mandapam* and place the pot in front of the *mandapam*. Then he washes the stone, which is placed in the *mandapam* as a symbol of *bagavathi*, with turmeric water. After that, the upper part of the stone is applied with the turmeric paste, and then a twenty-five or fifty paise coin is fixed on it.

One of the members of *tharavadu*, who receives the *dharshanam* of *bagavathi*, becomes the *velichapadu*. The person, who gets possessed, wears the red coloured dress, known as *chuvanna pattu* of *bagavathi* after getting *darshanam*. *Velichapadu* gives an order (*kalpana)* of the matters what they have to do. As part of the ritual the *velichapadu* cuts the head of *nercha kozh*i (offered hen) in front of the stone and drinks its blood. This indicates that the god will take away all their problems and take care of them. They believe that once *karivilly kariyathan* came to the forest as *malankuravan* and *malankurathi* and that they still live in the *Velloor mala* where nobody is allowed to go.

As mentioned earlier, once *karivilli kariyathan* seemed to have appeared in the form of *velichappadu* and given a *kalpana* (order). Accordingly, there are 18 *kadakams* (aboard of *karivillykariyathan*) in different parts of that forest, which must be sprayed with water all over and kept neat and clean. Among the 18 *kadakam*s 7 are important. They are:

1. Valathur
2. Peraty
3. Perunthattu
4. Payamuty
5. Thenevaram
6. Kottuthara
7. Pathilambalam

Other important sacred centres are in Kadachikkunnu, Chennayakolli, Munnoooru, Kadooru, Rippon, Pulloorpadi, Kottanad, Ambalavayal, Cheengavallam and Chembothara. In these centeres *karivilli karaiyathan* is worshiped. When *karivilli kariyathan* appeared in the forest as *malankuravan* and *malankurathi*. First, they seemed to have reached a place called *Neelimala, Neeliyamma* was the reigning deity. She seemed to have told them that they could not stay there, as she had to stay alone. Then she seemed to have shown the way to *kaarankudamala*, where *karankuda muthappan* was the reigning deity. He had also objected to their stay and showed the way to *Pathilambalam*. There, *karivilli kariyathan* and his *ezhuvillan* had stayed. There they had also danced. Their dance has become part of the folklore of Thachanadan Moopan as *thira*.

Karanavastanam

The term *karanavar* refers to the head of a family and the term *stanam* means position. Thus *karanavastanam* is indicating the position of the head of the *taharavadu* or *chali*. Thus it is found in the house of the head of tharavadu or in the house of the head of *chali*. The *moopan* is the head of the *tharavadu* and *chalithekkanam* is the head of the *chali*. Thus, the *karanavastanam* indicates the position (i.e., *moopan, lepan,* or *theakanam*). *Karanavastanam* indicates a small square-shaped platform in a room. The *kanayam* is also placed in this room. They believe that in the *kanayam*, the dead ancestors existed. The position of the *karanavar* is hereditary. With the changes in position, due to the death or the weak physical/mental condition of the existing position, the *karanavastanam* also changed from the house of old *moopan* to newly selected one. The *karanavastanam* is not transferred away from the territory. The place is considered sacred. Thus, the polluted people do not enter or touch the room. Delivery is not allowed in such houses. Some sacred performances such as *naming ceremony, chaalile oottu* or *vechoottal karmam* (food providing ceremony) are done in the room for the dead ancestors. In olden days, marriage and *kathukuthu* ceremonies are conduct only in these houses.

Kathukuthukallyanam (Ear boring ceremony)

Kathukuthu ceremony is one of the ceremonies performing in the *karanavasthanam*. Each boy and girl among the Thachanandan Moopan has to undergo the ear-boring ceremony in olden days. Only then, they are included in their group. This is compulsory at that time but now it is much relaxed. This ceremony is conducting as a group ceremony in the past. These ceremonies are held in the home of *karanavar,* in the room where the *kaaranavastanam* is settled. When a girl's *kathukuthu* ceremony is done, first she has to take bath in the stream, then wears the traditional dress called *thuni,* using a towel as a shawl in the shoulder. Eyebrows and eyelids are blackened with ink. For boys, a thread named *poonool* given by the *moopan* is tied across the body. All these are done in the *karanavastanam* room of the *karanavar*'s house. After this, the child is brought to the portico where they arrange a mat containing wooden plank, in front of which a glowing lamp and *naakkila* (plantains leaf) are placed. In that *naakkila* (plantain leaf), beaten rice, coconut, jaggery and cucumber are placed. The child goes around this mat three times. After this, one by one is called to stand up on that plank and their ears are pinned with a copper needle.

Then the child's father and mother pronounce the name to the *moopan* of the *tharavadu* and he calls the child by that name. At the same time, the parents holds the child at a height of 3 feet from the plank, and one coconut is broken above the child's head, allowing the water to fall on the child's head. The parents give *dakshina* (offering) to *pettichi* (midwife). At that time, they arrange a feast to all those who are present there in a full length plantain leaf. All the people have food in the same plantain leaf. This custom shows their unity and integrity.

Chaalile Ootu or *Vechoottu Karmam*

Thachanandan Moopan's have a ritual during the malayalam month of *karkitakam*. On the first day of *karkitakam* (July-August), they provide food to the ancestral spirits. This ritual is also called *vechootu karmam*. It is done only by males. In the morning, the *karanavar* who performs the ritual, takes bath and while returning, takes some water in a pot. Then he prepares the food out of rice. (They have the belief that this vessel could not touch the earth before taking in to plantain leaf). And it is taken directly to the leaf where the *padam* is placed. *Padam* represents ancestral spirits known as *tharmayam*. After sprinkling water 3 times he leaves the place and after sometimes, he returns to sprinkle water three times again, and takes back the food. This food is served to the women who do not have children. The *karanavar* also says "next time your child will come for this ritual". If this woman conceives a child, in the following year during this ritual she provides a silver figure of *chaali muthachi*. This figure is given in a basket and the *karanavar* puts it near the *kanayam*. It possessed by the person, who is the *moopan* of the *chali*.

Homestead

In certain houses, there is a practice to worship gods and goddesses nearby home. Before, they construct a *mandapam* (mud plat form) under a tree. In it, they place a stone of triangular shape. This triangular shape indicates the hills where they live and fulfill their daily life. They keep the place clean and neat. They light a *thiri* (lamp) at the place everyday evening and especially on Thursday and Friday other wise they believe that the gods become dissatisfied. When they start a new activity, they light a *thiri* in front of it. When they go for hunting, they pray before *gulikan* to get better hunt. They also consider *gulikan* as the *kavalkaran* (protector). They also construct special huts adjacent to the house of the *moopan* to preserve the *vala* (bangle) and *pattu* (shawl) of the Gods, as these sacred objects cannot be kept within the house. These are allowed to be kept in the temple only during festivals (*uthsavam*). Women are not allowed to enter into such abodes. It is not allowed to take non vegetarian food or meat or fish near this plce. Womens also not allowed to enter during the period of mensuration. The person who is with *pula* (death pollution) also not allowed to the place for a period of thirty days.

Pilgrim Centers

In olden times, the main pilgrim centres of Thachanadan Moopan include *Parassini kadavu* and *Shabarimala*. They also go to other temples.

Parassini kadavu: In olden times, they used to go to Parasini Kadavu and stay there. Parasini Kadavu is a temple where Lord Shiva is worshiping in childhood form. Now a day instead of *karanavastanam*, they go to parassinikadavu primarily for food initiation ceremony of their children.

Sabarimala: Shabarimala is the temple of Lord Ayyappa. They mainly go to Sabarimala to see *makaravilaku*. During the preparatory phase of 41 days before going to the Ayyappan temple on pilgrimage, the pilgrims who are known as *swamis* assemble in a nearby temple and sing songs of Lord Ayyappa every early morning and evening. From olden days some of the people of Thachandan Moopan went there with *thirumudi*. Only males go to that temple.

They take 41 days fasting. These persons are called *swami*. They eat rice food only once a day. Other time they eat vegetable foods like *chembu (Yam)*, roots etc along with black tea. On the day they leave for Sabarimala, they go to the temple in the morning, and offer articles for *pooja*. After the *pooja*, *Guru Swami* fills one side of the *kettu (*bundle*)* with *neythenga* (Ghee filled inside the dry coconut) and in the other side of the *kettu, the* family members put rice and money for the pilgrimage. The *Guru swami* keeps this *kettu* up on their head. After stepping out, he breaks the coconut held in his right hand. They go to *sabarimala* to see the *makara jyothi*.

They have a custom to take ash from 101 houses. They believe that only those who observe the fast sincerely can get ash from 101 houses. It indicates those who observe the fast sincerely will get the blessings from the ancestors. They also believe that if they observe their fasting strictly and conduct regular prayers, they could hold these ashes without getting their fingers burned. They also visit other temples like Kadampuzha, Thirupathi, etc.

Sacred Performance

The sacred performances are performed on special occasions by an individual or family or a group. Usually these performances are done by a special person; he may be a priest or shaman. Sacred specialists are the priest associated with different centres and help worshippers and pilgrims in the sacred performance (Srivastava 2007). She also says that they (shaman or priest) are religious headmen and are responsible for in which they have great influence and command. Shamans, commonly defined as intermediaries between the "natural" and "super- natural" worlds, communed with the supernatural through ritual and ecstatic trances to gain help and knowledge for healing, weather manipulation (e.g., rain seeking), divination, ensuring successful hunts, finding lost objects, self-empowerment, killing enemies, or other important activities such as ensuring fertility and fecundity for the benefit of their people (VanPool 2003: 696). Priests as members of the corporate structure who manipulate spirits, but unlike shamans do not become them. Priests hold full-time office whereas shamans are conceptualized as being part-time religious practitioners. In the real world religious practitioners often employ attributes of both (Miller and Taube 1993:152), becoming shaman-priests. One of the important components of the Sacred Complex of the tribals is sacred performance, mainly performed by the village priest and/or his assistant. The main thing in this respect for the tribal is the sacrifice to propitiate the god or deity. The sacred performances reflect the method of propitiation, rituals, worship, offering sacrifice etc. adopted by the people (Vidyarthi 1976:328).

Festivals (*Utsavam*)

Utsavam of Thachanandan Moopan is generally conducted during *meenam* and *medam* (March-May) in Malayalam month and are mainly confined today to the important temples such as *Pathilambalam*, and *Valathur Kaavu*. In olden days, there was a fixed date to conduct *utsavam*. *Meenam* (Mey) 25 at Peraty, *Meenam* (Mey) 26 at Thenavarm, *Meenam* (Mey) 27 at Valathur, Meenam (Mey) 28 at Perunthattu, *Meenam* (Mey) 29 at Payamudi, Meenam (Mey) 30 at Kottathara and *Medam* 1(Mey) at Pathailambalam. It is also noted that there are differences in rituals in these sacred grooves.

In olden days, all the functions were conducted by the *tharavadu moopan* of the particular *kaavu*. Today, the economic problem has forced them to hand over these *kaavu* to the people's committee. The main problem is the increasing economic expenditure and due to the increasing population etc. They are dispersed in different parts and they can't bring everybody for this function, increasing price for the materials that they needed doing rituals are also other reasons. In olden days these products they got from the forest. But now the forest laws didn't allow them to take anything from the forest. The committee members include both Thachanandan Moopan and non–Thachanandan Moopan members. *Utsavam* is the only sacred occasion when they avoid worshipping dead ancestors.

Utsavam in Pathilambalam

Pathilambalam belongs to two *tharavadu*'s namely, *Lekarukaru* and *Moothlukaru*. The *Moopan* is always from the *Moothlukaru tharavadu while* the *Lepan* is always from the *Lekarukaru*. Thus, the *utsavam* is always conducted under the co-operation of both the groups. The custom is that even if the festival is initiated by one of these groups, there should atleast be a child from the other group in order to perform the ritual i.e. with the absence of other group one group alone can't do the rituals. For doing this rituals one child from another group is enough.

When they decide to conduct the festival and fix the date of the festival, first they put one *seru* (measure) of rice in front of the god in plantain leaf. This is to get the consent of the god to conduct festival and clear the *kaavu. Moopan* takes *kanayam* and *lepan* takes *pattu* and *valu*. Each group comes in front of the *mandapam* of *karivilli kariyathan*. Then first *moopan* put the *vadi* (stick) in front of the *mandapam* of *karivilli kariyathan* as he is the supreme deity. Then *leapn* put *vala* and *pattu* (which is considered as the cloth and weapon of the *bagavathi*) in front of the *manadapam* of *bagavathi. Moopan* is the officiating priest among the Thachanandan Moopan. In the absence of official functionaries, the elderly persons who are knowledgeable about the rituals can perform the rituals.

The festival begins with the lighting of the lamp on a mud platform called *mandapam*. Thachanandan Moopan put a plantain leaf in front of the *mandapam* of the *karivilli kariyathan*. On the left side of the plantain leaf are placed beaten rice, banana, kalkandi, munthiri, sandal and oil and on the right side are placed raw rice, cucumber and a coconut. This is called *ilayum ilathanavum*. First, it should be given to *karivilli kariyathan*. Only then it is given to other gods. At that time the oracle (*velichapadu*) becomes spirit-possessed. Then the *moopan* says to *velichapadu* "*Onne mukkaaal nazhika kondu vannu paranju tharanam, ilayum ilathanavum vechitundu*" (I put *ilathanam* (plantain leaf with raw rice, cucumber and a coconut) for, you should come and tell with in 15 minutes).

Then the *velichapadu* takes *kanayam* and runs three or four times infront of the mandapam. Then he says "*ee kurukkan sthanathu kunjanum kuttiyuum ente aavashyathinu vanni, enne enthinu vilichu peraka, nee oradi vechal njan pathadi munnilundavum*" (All of you have come here for my purpose. Why did you call me? I am always with you in any situation). Then all of them get remedies for their problems and receive wishes and blessings from the god. After this, the *thira* of *karrivilli kariyathan*, *gulikan*, and *bagavathi* are performed. They give the *prasadam* to the devotees. The *prasadam* of *karivilli kariyathan* is *kari* (burnt fuel wood) mixed with oil, whereas *gulikan* gives turmeric powder as *prasadam* and *bagavathi* give flowers. There is a *nagathara* in that *kaavu*. Thachanandan Moopan gives coconut also as *nercha* (offering).

Kambakuth Kalyanam or Puta Kalyanam

The *karanavar*'s from 36 *tharavadu* participate in this ceremony. This programme continues for 7 days. From 36 *tharavadu*s, one *tharavadu* is selected to conduct this function. The *karanavar*s from 36 *tharavadu* fix the day to celebrate. The ceremony is controlled by *karimi* and *manackam*. Twelve people including *karimi, manakam* (religious functionaries) *moopan and lepan* participate in this *kambakuth kalyanam*. All of them take *Vratham* for 7 days during which they take bath two times, didn't eat anything from outside. They avoid meat, fish and sexual relations.

The very first day all the people go to bamboo forest and select a bamboo cluster with good condition and quality. Then, they clean the cluster and purify it all around with cow dung mixed in water. Then one among them goes to trance locally called *urayal* and finally, he selects one good quality bamboo from the cluster. Others take away the bamboo cutting it above the ground level. After that, they cut the bamboo to size, keeping 12 nodes on it. Then they bring it to the *tharavadu* keep it in a place. They use seven colours known as *chanthupottu* and colour the bamboo. This bamboo is known as *omakkaal*. A lamp is lighted in front of it. They have a seven days feast to all the members reaching there. They also give fruits, beetle nuts etc. to all those who visit them. They conduct the play for seven days. They play their traditional dance, known as *omakkali,* keeping the bamboo known as *omakal* at the center. They sing songs with drums, *udukku, thudi, chenda* etc. They play at evening time. The women and men play separately around the *omakal* forming two circles, the men in the inner circle and the women in the outer circle. On the last day, they play for more time. *Velichapadu* also takes place on the same day. This indicates that their ancestral spirits are satisfied and came to give blessings. Nowdays, this ceremony is not celebrated for want of money to meet the expenditure.

Ritual during the Selection of New Karanavar

When a head *(moopan/lepan)* in a *tharavadu* died, the *Kanayam* put down words as a symbol of condolence to the died person, till the celebration of *adiyanthiram* day. After the funeral, they wash the *kanayam* and make coral marks on a spot with a knife. This coral mark shows the ending of one *moopan-stanam* (position) and starting another one. After starting *adiyanthiram*, on the 3rd day, the 36 *padi karanavar*s select a list of members from the dead *karanavar's* padi. The list may contain up to 10-15 members. Then it is left to the *velichapadu* to select one person from the list as the next *karanvar*. They spread a mat, and a cleaned mortar is put facing downward. They place the *kanayam* on it. At that time, everyone stands and chant prayer to gods *karivilly kariyathan, gulikan, bagavathi* and to the ancestors saying *"Ninte vazhchayku venti nee thane nalla oral thiranjedukkum"* (For your own goodness, you yourself select the best). Then the spirits appears to a person who becomes the *velichappadu*. He calls a person from the list and says, *"Ningal kandathalla unjanum kandathalla melkarnavar kanda poomaram aanu njan vekkan pokunnathu. makkalkku ellavarkum thripthiyayo?"* (The person that I have selected is not the one that you have selected but the one selected by the supreme. Are you satisfied?)

Then, *velichapadu* takes the selected person in front of the *kanayam* and places it on his head. That time, all the persons surround it and throw flowers and rice on him. Then the *velichapadu* says: *'Evane moopanaayi/lepanaayi thiranjeduthathu')*. This is the person who has been elected as *moopan/lepan*).

Karpa Pooja

This ritual is mainly intended to propitiate the deity *gulikan* performed in houses and sacred groves. For doing this ritual they arrange twenty squares at equal size made out of plantain leaf. He puttung this twenty one *narukku* made out of plantain leaf and twenty one lamps also putting infront of the *gulikan mandapam* in a round shape.In either sides of the *kalam* two-plantain leaves are kept. On the plantain kept on the right side, cucumber and coconut are placed & on the plantain kept on the left side, *beaten rice, malar*, jaggari and coconut are placed. These are kept on the *gulikan mandapam* (plat form). On the *gulikan thara* (platform) one *padam* (like a vessel) is made from a plantain leaf. Water mixed with turmeric and lime is kept in that padam. Toddy *(liquor)* is kept on the left plantain leaf and *appam* (a kind of food made out of rice) on the right. Then one among them gets possessed. The *velichapadu* cuts the head of the chicken and drinks its blood. He also puts a few drops of blood in the *padam* symbolically giving to the deity. After cooking the chicken, the right side of the *kuraku* (leg portion) is taken out and put on the right side of the *gulikan thara* on a plantain leaf. *Appam* (food) and liquor are also put on separate plantain leaves and are kept on the left side and middle of the *thara* respectively. All these are covered properly with a plantain leaf. Then the Moopan burns *sambrani* and chants prayers. Then he sprinkles some fresh water on it 3 times, believing that this devotion is for *gulikan*. Afterwards, he sprinkles water 3 times, and takes back and give it to all. This ritual is done for the wellbeing of the family and community.

Kallivettal

This ceremony is performed to eradicate evil spirits. The performance of this ceremony is known as *sheelthikkaran*. *Sheelthikkaran* draws a *kalam* using rice powder for white, dust of *Amarku* (a tree) leaf for green, and the mixing of turmeric, *chunnambu* (lime) and rice powder for red. They fill the *kalam* with different colours graphically. The total numbers of columns are 49 and this is square-shaped. Then the person who is posessed is seated infront of the *kalam*. From the *kalam, sheelthikaran* takes 49-lighted lamps each one kept in a small pot made of clay, around the head of the diseased person and the mouth of the pot is covered with a white cloth. Then, the pot is left in a flowing river. They believe that by doing this, the witches go out of the body.

Ceremony related to Kanayam, when it fell down

Kanayam is a wood stick. They believe that their ancestors live in it. When the *kanayam* falls down to the earth, they believe that their gods fall down to earth, and go beneath the soil. If it falls down, the *karimi* and *manakam* would take *vrutham* (fasting) for 7 days, during which they using only vegetarian food. They spread a mat at *karanavastanam* and put a peacock feather, and near by it 7 *padams* containing cooked rice are placed. Then *karimi* and *manakam* shake the two bells and chant mantras. Then the ancestral spirits appears in the body of *karimi* or *manakam*. They believe that when they are chanting in a dancing mood, the dust that rises from the earth is considered to the spirits comes from earth. Then they could take the *kanayam* that is lying on the floor and hang on the roof with a hope that the spirits are appeared and bless them.

Muttu arackura

This ceremony is performed generally at *moopan's* home. When any external force that is not within his control troubles a person, this ceremony is performed. This is done for curing the disease is any part of the body. The person who knows this ritual does this. They go to the temples like Kadampuzha temple, Thirupathi etc. and perform this. When a troubled person does this, he brings along with him three sets of beetle leaves and beetle nut, one coin, and coconut. The one who performs the ritual spreads a mat and arranges all things in the mat. Then he performs the ritual, putting the last part of the plantain leaf for lighting a lamp. Then he measures the length of the troubled person with a thread and rolls it seven times, equally. The rolled thread is soaked in the coconut oil and put on an unbroken coconut. Then, this coconut is taken around his body three times and broken in front of him. Thus they believe that all the evils in his body disappear.

Rituals performed on different occasions

Apart from the sacred performances, the community has other rituals too. These rituals are performed at individual, family, and community levels. Some such rituals include those related to farming, rituals related to house construction, rituals on the occasion of selecting a new *karanavar*, etc.

Rituals related to House Construction

In olden days, they did not have any rituals related to house construction. First, they prepare the materials (bamboo, clay, creeper, mud bricks and grass) to construct the house from the forest. And they find a suitable time, which is convenient for all for undertaking construction work. Now days, they first go to the *panikkar* to find the position of their star and submit it to *moopan*. That day *moopan* calls the carpenter and fixes the *kutti* (stick) to construct the house. At that time, they perform pooja to the ancestoral spirits. First, they make *kavayi* (foundation) and lay the store *kotikallu* (new stone) eastward. They leave a coin under the *kotikallu*. On the house-warming day, all family members take bath; come inside the new house, light a lamp and burn agarbathi, to propitiate their ancestral spirits. That day, *ganapathi pooja* is also performed along with *kuttupooja/aduppu pooja*. Then coconut is broken in the hearth and milk is boiled. However, in the past, such practices were not prevailed among them. The front portion of every house is built eastward, so that they can see the sun God in the morning. They construct the room for *karanavastaanam* at northwest corner. The kitchen is in the west side.

Rituals related to Farming

In olden days, they practiced shifting cultivation. The *Moopan* would start cutting the trees and bushes in the four corners. Then all of them would join the *moopan*. Then *moopan* would put fire on it. During sowing, *lepan* would dig the earth, and *moopan* would sow the first seed. Afterwards, every body would join him. During harvesting, they would take a handful of paddy, put it in the leaf of *avanakam* (a tree) and bury it under the soil. After harvesting, the buried paddy is crushed and offered to the gods as they believe that gods have given them good harvest.

Kathiretuckal chatangu (Harvesting ceremony)

This ceremony is being performed at the time of first harvesting. This is done on the 10th day of the Malayalam month *thulam* (Oct-Nov). As *moopans* worked in the field of *wayanadan chetty,* on this day, they would take out a few bunches of paddy, ragi, *chama* and tie them together and would go to the temple of the landlord, which was also their temple then. Infront of the temple, they would hang down this bunch. Then they would go to the landlord's home and repeat the same. There they would get food and feast. After this, they would reach their *karanavar's* (*moopan*) house. There, one mat would be placed in front of their hut, and a clean mortar is placed on it, facing downward. Then they put one of the bunches on it. After this, it would be supplied to every family and would be hung down in every house. The *karanavar* also hang this down in front of the house, and in the room of *karanavasthanam*. The ceremonies are performed by the *moopan* of the *tharavadu*. Before performing this, he undergoes fasting for seven days, without consuming non-vegetarian food.

Spirit possession

The term spirit possession generally denotes the incarnation or possession of individual by some vague external forces. According to culture the spirit may possess or control the individual person in a number of different ways- it may reside in the head, 'ride' the individual as a horse, or a spirit might fully incarnate the person, taking full control over his body – and a person is 'seized' by the divinity or spirit. He or she becomes a 'vessel' or a temple on the embodiment of the spirit (Spiro 1987).

The Thachanadan Moopan have the practice of spirit possession. There are several reasons behind the spirit possessions. It is mainly during occasions of festivals, when a new karanavar is to be selected. If a problem has to be solved, Thachanadan Moopan calls for *velichappadu* in the house, to understand the causes of troubles or diseases in the house. The velichapadu come to the house after bathing in the stream. The *moopan* of the *tharavadu* receives him by giving *pattu* and *valu* (cloth and sword). After wearing this dress, the *velichapadu* prays to the gods, goddesses and ancestral spirits. After a while he/she gets *darshanam*. Then comes to give orders and solutions for their problems.

Folk-plays during ceremonial occasions

They perform a number of folk plays and songs such as *kolkali adiyanthirakali, vattakali* related to sacred performances. The dancing and singing express their happiness during the occasion.

Kolkali and Vattakkali

Kolkali is a traditional dance played by the men-folk. This is performed mainly on the occasion of marriage ceremony. The play is around a *nilavilaku* (lighted lamp). They stand in round at a certain distance -with wooden sticks in the hands. The sticks they use are approximately one feat long. The dance performers move in a circle striking small sticks and keeping rhythm with special step. The circle expands and contracts as the dance progress. The accompanying music gradually rises in pitch and the dance reaches its climax. At the time of play, they sing songs according to Ramayana or Mahabharata epics.While playing the players themselves singing the song. First one person start to sing and others repeat the same line. The song and the sounds of the stick while beating each other produce a good music for the song and play. *Vattakali* is a type of play, done only by the males. It is conducted during *ulsavam* and marriage occasions.

Adiyanthirakali

This is played at the time of *thira* or *utsavam*. Only the women play this, Five to eight members join the play. They perform the *pooja* in a temporarily constructed shelter, before starting the play in front of the *nilavilaku*. They play in circular movement. They have step on legs in uniform movement and hit the hand at each other, making a uniform sound.

Kurathi Natakam

It is a play conducted during summer. The play is based on the Hindu epic 'Ramayana'. It includes stories and songs. The music instruments they use are *chenda* and *ilathalam*. The males play the roles of women (*kurathi*) in the play.

3

CHANGING TRENDS AND PERSISTING TRADITIONS

The word 'change' denotes a difference in anything observed over some period of time. It is nonsense to say that any society is in equilibrium all are in process of constant change (Mair 1971: 270). What is today shall be different from what it would be tomorrow, therefore change is the law of nature. Social change has occurred in all societies and in all periods of time hence there will be differences in any social phenomena after a time period. Inshort social change means to any cyclical modifications in the group or society that changes the earlier traditional one and introduces a new one. These changes are visible in the social relations, institutions, behavoural patterns, organisations etc. Nordskog (1960:31-6) accounts certain processes which accountable to social change. First of all, there is a process by which an organism becomes adapted to a new climate which he refers *to acclimatization.* Then there is the *accommodation* process, which involves a functional change in the habits and customs of persons and groups and, by this old habits are given up and new habits formed. Social change also involves a process of organization, i.e., the gradual development of an integrated scheme of structures and functions suited to a rather definite mode of life under specific conditions. This is called adaptation. People of diverse racial origins and different cultural heritages occupying a common territory tend to be similar alike. By this process people acquire the language of the immigrated people gradually participated in the economic political and social activities thus becoming assimilated. Thus they become culturally similar to their neighbours and form part of a cultural solidarity. This process is known as assimilation.

According to Moore (1968:366) social change is the significant alteration of social structure (that is, of patterns of action, social and interaction), including consequences and manifestations of such structure embodied in norms (rules of conduct), values, cultural products and symbols. In this point of view any alteration to be socially significance has to be accepted by the people and has to be assimilated or integrated in the society. Martindale (1962) discussed the functionalist theory of change as two types such as exogenous and endogenous. An exogenous factor arises outside the social system, where as the endogenous factor is internal to the social system. Anthropologists established the terms like culture contact, cultural shock, enculturation and acculturation to illustrate the cultural changes and its modifications with the incorporation as well as the expulsion of cultural traits, behavioural patgterns etc. to the indigenous life. Acculturation is the state when a number of cultures came into contact and it results in the alteration of its original form. Moore (1965) points out the chief modes of acculturation as imperialism, wars, conquests, missionary religions, mass migration, individual migration, trade tourism, transported labour, transfer of knowledge, formal communications, etc. Nordscog (1960) understanding of social change is through the process of borrowing cultural elements from contemporary cultures by the process of adoption, an act of taking and applying something or putting into practices originally.

Social change can also occur with the process of duiffusion by which one can adopt and replicate ideas or practices or beliefs by which cultural traits spread from one culture to another. This is the process which reflects the idea of 'continuam' in the cultural traits of near by areas. Barnabas (1967) states that a number of aspects results in the social change and they produce a cumulative affect on any particular situation. Changes taking place with the result that over a period of time changes taking place in certain aspects become more perceptible than others. Vasudeva (1976) found the important factor responsible for social change is political organisation where as family structure, religious beliefs and practices are supposed to have remarkable stability and power of resistance against the focus of change.

Invention and discovery occurred in different parts of the world are also involved in the process of social change. Discovery of new facts or principles presupposes the invention of new methods of acting or thinking which results in to new culture traits. The traditional religion of Thachanadan Moopan is in the way of change with the changing time. Those changes are mainly in the settlements which are nearer to the mainstream people. In the dense forest they are struggling for food and protection from the animals. Thus one would call all his supernatural powers, spirits and deities to protect him. In the changed environment also he is suffering from starvation. Thus to cope up with this problems he fell back to his old beliefs and practices.

Srinivas (1952) put forward the concept oof Sanskritisation to discuss the changes occurred in the religious life of Indian society especially of Hinduism. The concept of sanskritization represent the process by which a low hindhu caste or tribal or other group changes its custom, rituals, ideology and way of life in the direction of height and frequency twice born caste. In the view of srinivas, the people are converting themselves by adapting the customs, rituals, etc. of the superior or the higher caste to show their superiority over others or to be equal. With the support of the concept of 'diffusion', Srinivas (1952) introduced the concept 'spread' to discuss the ways of spreading Hinduism i.e. vertically and horizontally. Vertical spread refers to the Brahmins in any linguistic area, share some cultural and ritual forms with all castes including the lowest in that area and by Horizontally meant to Brahmins everywhere in India, have much sanskritic rituals in common irrespective of geographical and linguistic diversities. Upadhyay (1993) defined diffusion as the process by which culture traits, discovered or invented at one place or society, are spread directly or indirectly to other societies or places. Although the exact origin of specific cultural traits is difficult to trace, but diffusion of a trait fairly be traced.

Singh (2003) mentioned that the census data on tribals religion have never been exactly comparable, the number of tribal following their religion declined by 33percent between 1921 and 1931. It declined from roughly one third (18.2 million) of the tribal people in 1931 to about 6 percent in 1981, with Hinduism claiming 87 percent and Christianity 7 percent and adherent among tribals. The census of India 2001 shows that the Scheduled Tribes professing Hinduism account for 93.7 per cent. Christian tribals are 5.8 per cent while less than half per cent of tribal follow Islam and religion not stated. Thachanadan Moopan has varying contact with other religions. Their contact with Hindus is very intimate as they are the largest neighbours in the settlement, while their contact with Christians is limited. The Muslim contacts in the study settlements are negligible. Thus we can see the impact of Hindus and Christians, i.e. the process of Hinduisation and Christianisation, on the Thachanadan Moopan is a sure possibility.

Hinduization

Menon (2003) discussed Hinduisation as the process that involves sharing of a belief system, of which belief in the reincarnation of soul, the sanctity of Veda, however unknown and unapproachable they be to the believer, and the acceptance of the pre eminence of the brahmin as the agency between god and man have been essential features. Rapid hinduisation has been going on the greater part of the tribes willingly proclaim Hinduism as their religion, use Hindu names, celebrate Hindu temples (Kattakayam 1983: 40). In the study settlement out of the 50 households 30 households claim to be Hindus. The Thachanadan moopan traditionally believe in their supreme god *Karivillikariyathan*. Now they believe that *Karivilli kariyathan* is the incarnation of lord Siva and Parvathi, the Hindu gods. They also believe in other Hindu gods such as *ganapathi, subramaniam, kali* etc. Hindu Gods appear in the houses through wall calenders and pictures. But they are kept for their aesthetic values more than as an object of worship. Belief in the witchcraft and sorcery is declining but belief in the ancestral spirits, and taboos are not much declined. Education economic security and availability of modern medical facilities are the breaking factors of age old beliefs. When the tribal section becomes more hinduised, becomes ashamed of its habits and customs and tries to deny or conceal them. This sense of inferiority is perhaps the best indicator of a transformation of a tribal group into a caste since it denotes a loss of its dignity, its pride its sense of equality and its independence (Kattakayam 1983: 82).

Nowadays they started to construct small temples. And they also started worshiping in a manner similar to that of Brahminical tradition by fixing a *poojari* (a person from a *namboothiri* caste who performing rituals) to perform the ceremonies. Thus the role of *moopan* and *lepan* as religious functionaries is declining. By worshiping at the common centers they are getting social relations. By leaving these sacred beliefs and centers they will lose social membership and religious affiliation through clan ties. (Kattakayam 1983: 85). In the case of Hinduisation nobody is inspiring or forcing them to accept Hindu Gods and Goddesses, instead some factors such as to come upward in the social stratum, and to be equal with the other plains people they have to imitate them because they are surrounded by the vast environment of Hinduism, which often belittles tribal people. There is the inferiority complexion created their mind that they are worshiping the sticks (*kanayam*) is also one of the factor that compelled them to accept the higher caste and their manner of worshipping. Nowadays they perform rituals and ceremonies of Hindus like house warming ceremonies, *ehuthiniruthuka*, (the initiation ceremony related to education) siva rathri, Shri Krishna jayanthi associated with Hindu gods. On this regard we can see the impact of mass media which reflects and personify Hindu mythology and deities respectively. Even though the older generation people are illiterate they are watching TV and understood the Hindu epics. Thus mass media playing an important role in the conversion to Hinduism.

Christianisation

Jain's (1955) study on Christianity ideology and social change among tribes provide the reason of the Bhils taking the Christianity in their appealing poverty in being discriminated against by the sawarna Hindu and degradation. They seemed children of a lesser god. Christianity promised them relative prosperity, end of discrimination and social upliftment and dignity. Sahay (1976) studied the impact of Christianity especially among the Oraons of Chotanagpur to understand the structural change happened in such a society. He suggests some cultural processes such as oscillation, scrutinization, combination, indigenization and Retroversion when some new faith enters into traditional society. Cultural oscillation is a process that has a certain amount of instability and suggest a sort of fluctuation between two essentially opposed set of ideals and values belonging to two different sections". The process of cultural scrutinization leads to elimination and retention of tribal traditions by the converts. This process is followed by cultural combination. Which is described as the mixing of up or a combination of the saran elements with newly introduced Christian elements. For example, tribal dancing is organised on the occasions like Easter, Christmas etc. According to Sahay cultural indigenisation is a specialised type of combination and in context with a specified beliefs or practice it implies a partial replacement of sarna elements with functionally similar Christian elements. Cultural retroversion is the revaluation of previously eleminated sarna elements and their readoption after necessary modification to suit the changed needs and outlook of the converts.

Converted tribal got ample help from the missionaries with regard to education, medical facilities etc. But the missionaries were able to disintegrate the tribal Christian from their original societies and customs (Sen 2005: 35). Thus conversion was a result of the reasonable adjustment made by people on the basis of this evaluation of rival religious beliefs (Robinson 1998:32). Conversion to Christianity is reported among the Thachanadan Moopans of Wayanad. There are nine families consisting of 42 members (26 males and 16 females) converted to Pentecostal denomination of Christianity.

They have their own way of worshipping, life cycle rituals and way of life when compared to the traditional Thachanadan Moopan and the hinduised Thachanadan Moopan. Hinduised Thachanadan Moopan are still practicing ancestral worship, rituals and ceremonies. Thus we can see the process of syncretism. Syncretism has been defined as the attempted reconciliation or union of different or opposing principles, practices, as in philosophy of religion (Menon 2003: 119). But Christianised Thachanadan Moopans are leaving idol worship, ancestral worship, superstitious beliefs etc. They abstain all the formal rituals and the use of the *thulasi* leafs, rice flour, oil, flowers, use of betel leaves for the ceremonial purposes were prohibited. Christianised Thachanadan Moopan not at all using any kind of jewels or ornaments.

One of the important ceremonies in the life of the Christianized Thachanadan Moopan is the *Jnanasnanam* (Baptism). The word baptism derived from the batizeen meaning to dip in to the water. Baptism is thus literally means immersion or sprinkling of water as a religious ceremony. Baptism is a sacrament by which the recipient is solemnly admitted to membership of Christ's holy church and there after grafted in to his physical body (Sholparker 1990: 111). It is believed that a person can baptize only when he/she understood and accept the way and words of Jesus Christ. Thus baptism is applicable to the person who understood about Jesus Christ and his words. It was a ritual performed by the church on this occasion, in the morning the person to be baptized, his family, relatives, friends and the church members go to a stream. The pastor and devotee enter in to the stream, the Pastor pray. Then the pastor led the person to immerse in the stream.

The marriage ceremony is very simple. In most of the cases marriage proposal are coming through the Church. If both the parties like they fix the date of the marriage in the home itself. Before the date of marriage three Sunday's bride and bridegroom should be there in the church during prayer time. If the bride and bride groom are from distant villages it is not necessary to come to the same church, instead bride goes to her church and groom go to his church. That time pastor make a public announcement asking to the people whom ever gathered there, marriage is fixed between this boy and girl (name of the boy, girl and their parents mentioned), is any body have any objection against it. It was done in the church initiated by Pastor. Marriage ceremony goes to 2 to 3 hours. First the pastor praying then the people gathered there sing song. After that, Bibles are exchanged between both bride and groom. Bride didn't wear any jewels because the penthacostal belief system did not allow it. After that everybody clapping and singing the songs. Then the pastor read a chapter from the Bible. Then both bride and groom putting sign by saying I will be with him/ her till my death.

Every Sunday they are gathering in the church. It is called Sunday service. Pastor starting with a small prayer. After that those gathered singing songs praising Jesus Christ.

Then the pastor sings the song and others repeating the song with clapping. Again pastor read a chapter of proverb from the Bible. Next those whom ever felt good things in their life through the prayer share to everybody. This providing mental purification and satisfaction to the people.

Their important festivals are Christmas and Easter. They are celebrating both Easter and Christmas day. According to Christian scripture, Jesus was resurrected from the dead on the third day from his crucifixion i.e. two days after Good Friday. Christians celebrate this resurrection on Easter Day or Easter Sunday. On the day they are singing songs related to Easter. Pastor give message related to Easter.

Christmas Day, is an annual holiday celebrated on December 25 that commemorates the birth of Jesus. On Christmas day morning four 'o' clock they go to church. In the beginning they give a starting prayer, then sing three or four songs about Jesus. After that they sing a worship song. Then they give offering to the church. It may be money or gold, depends up on the person. Then there is drama or skit by the youth and the children. After that Pastor give the Christmas message, specially from Mathew, Mark, Luke, John (from New Testament) and Isharia and Jeromiah (Old testament). After that they are singing silent night song with a candle in the hand. Then they cut the cake and distributing chocolates. At last they are says 'Aameen' and disperse from the church.

These are unbearable for the traditional Thachanadan Moopan, while they have good relation with hinduised

Thachanadan Moopan. Thus they never allow the Christianized Thachanadan Moopan to join and participate in the activities of the Thachanadan Moopan. Because they are working and participating in other religious group rituals and ceremonies and functions. They are not obeying the rules of the Moopan instead they are going and asking advices from the Pastor and other church members. It was great insult for the traditional people. Thus they are keeping distance from the Christianized people. It is also believed that Christianized people not at all worshiping and propitiating the ancestral spirits and supernatural. They are not keeping any purity concept. Thus they may get the wrath of the god and also those that interact with them. Thus traditional people are keeping distance with the Christian Thachanadan Moopan.

The missionaries come to villages and preaching about Jesus Christ. Most of them converting to Christianity because of their faith in the Jesus Christ. In some cases the pastor pray for the people whom ever with physical and mental disturbances. Their diseases get cured. This makes others to believe that Christianity as real path. They believing that if they join to Christianity their problems will get solve. Whom ever interested they can join in the Christianity. As these Christianised ThachanadanMoopan are kept away from all the social activities of the unconverted Thachanadan Moopan.The converted people created their own group joining with other caste and tribe members who have become Christians. Many sections of different tribes come together under the same religious leadership and the network of church (Sundar 2001:264).

Those could not sustain huge sacrifices and offerings to the Gods and spirits go to the churches and offer with out any sacrifice. Such prayers gave them mental as well as spiritual satisfaction. If we ask the reason they will say that conversion is due to their faith in Jesus Christ. They also believe that they can get rid of alcoholic addiction once converted to Christianity. Poverty is also a factor for the religious conversion. In the case of Thachanadan Mooapan they didn't have permanent income. The missionaries being supplied with new cloths during festival time, medicines and services as a help to the poor families. They are also helping during the marriage occasion and house construction, if the family is not financially capable. Education another factor, due to the close contact with the outsiders they are now interested to giving education to their children. Even though the govt. providing stipends and all it's not enough for a family for the whole year. Thus missionaries giving of new dress, books etc make them to go the way of Christianity. They are also giving medicines through medical camps, not only to the converted but to all people whomever coming. Converted Christian's social life is fully related with church. As because the non Christianized people rejecting them in social life they are more and more attracted to the church life.

The Thachanadan Moopans say that they do not maintain any contact with the converted people. They are not allowed to participate in any of the life cycle rituals of Thachanadan Moopan. They treat them as another group. The converted creating themselves as new endogamic group by marrying with in the penthacostals. But in such cases there is no geographical boundary. They can marry any penthacostal in any where in the world.

Case of a Converted Family

Appu (60) and Kamala (51) are husband and wife. They have 3 children namely Sreeju (30), Sreejih (28), Shanti (29). Appu lost his parents in his child hood itself. So he did not know the ceremonies exactly. Close to his house, an old man Chappen was living. He was the Moopan of the *tharavadu*. He stayed lonely without any family member. One of his daughters was married to a person in a nearby village. As per their community custom, the position of Chappen should not go to his daughter's *tharavadu*. So he decided to give his position to Appu. Chappan stayed with Appu for one and a half years and also requested to take Moopan's Kanayam. But Appu did not agree because there was another elder member (Achappan) in Appu's *tharavadu* to take this position. He was staying in another *tharavadu* as he had his property in that *tharavadu*/ Further, as per their custom, Kanayam should not be taken to another tharavadu. Thus, Appu could not take this position. So, Chappen got angry and went to his daughter's home. After one week, he returned to Appu's home. After four days he died. The cause of his death was attributed to Appu.

On the day of *adiyanthiram,* the problem was raised in *karimbadam*. Then Achappan took the position of *moopan* and Appu took the position of *lepan*. Both of them performed all the ceremonies. At that time, Appu's friend Peter invited him to the assembly of prayer. Appu called his wife also to go. Kamala did not allow him because she thought about family customs and rules. But Appu told her that he was going to the prayer and she could not live there without his permission. Then she thought about the situations and went with him once. She witnessed the prayer and service was attracted to join the congregation and conined to attend prayer afterwards also. But their own society members did not like it and they asked him to return the *kanayam* and they took it immediately. So they joined the Pentecostal sect.

In the case of Appu, as he Christianised he is not allowed to participate in the rituals and ceremonies including social life. After converting to Penthacostal sect he didn't perform the rites and rituals as a Thachanadan Moopan. But every week he is going to the Church. After the conversion he treated the pastor as in the position of the Moopan. We can conclude that the basic causes of conversion appear to be the desire for improvement in the standard of living and social status through conversion.

4

SUMMERY AND CONCLUSION

Thachanadan Moopan is a tribe, mainly found in the Wayanad district of Kerala. In wayanad they are mainly concentrated in the viallages like Kadachikkunnu, Kottanadu, Rippon, Kallumala, Kunnambatta of Vythiri taluk and Ratakolli, Cheengollam, Chennayakkoli, Kunnamangalamvayal of Batheri taluk. Now a days they are spreading other parts of Wayanad also. The total population of Thachanadan Moopan in Kerala is 3000. They are brought under ST category only in 2003. Before that they belong to the OEC (Other Eligible Caste) category. The name Thachanadan Moopan is reported to have originated from their place of origin *Thachanad* (Maralusiddiah 2002: 1381). The present study is conducted in few a villages of Wayanad such as Kadachikkunnu, Kottanadu, Kallumala and Cheengollam.

The political orgnisations plays an important role in cultural and traditional life of *Thachanadan Moopan*. There are mainly two social divisions i.e. *'tharavadu'* and *'kulam'*. There seemed to have existed 36 *ttharavadu* and 101 *Kulam* in the past. At *tharavadu* level *moopan* and *leppan* are important persons holding authority. At *kulam* level *'thekkanam'* is the supreme authority. *Tharavadu* is patrilineal and *Kulam* is matrilineal. The *moopan, leppan* and *thekkanam* play an important role in socio religious and political functions. Their main function is to maintain social order. The position of *moopan* and *leppan* is hereditary and *thekkanam* is selected by oracle. The punishment is based on the crime. Killing was the severe punishment existed in the past which is known as *odimarichil*. Changes in the traditional political organization occurred due to the modern political parties. It plays an important role in the welfare of the community. At present, the power of traditional authorities decreased as compared to the past.

As Scheduled Tribe Thachanadan Moopan have their own belief system. Many sacred objects identified in the settlements of Thachanadan Moopan. Important one is *kanayam*. *Kanayam* is made out of branches from ack fruit (*Artocarpus heterophyllus*) tree. It is dangled in the corner of the room along with peacock feathers, usually the *kanayam* is kept on the deer horn and that is tied in the roof. The room, where the *kanayam* is kept, is known as *karanavastanam*. Another one is the representations of deities are done by Thachanadan Moopan using stone. Instead of Idols they utilize stones. Usually they use stones of triangular form, as they believe that, it represents or symbolizes the mountain, their dwelling place. The stones representing their deities are placed in mud platforms, which are called as *mandapam*. They believe, *Val* (Sword) is the weapon of *bagavathi*. The sword is made out of iron and brass. Hence they observe it as a sacred object. It is not allowed to be kept either in the house or in the sacred groves; it is kept in a separate hut with in the settlement. It is also permissible to keep it in the temple only during *uthsavam* (festivals) times. While getting the possession of *bagavathi* they use the weapon to symbolize that he or she is possessed by *bagavathi*. *Pattu*, a red coloured cloth, is also considered as the clothing of *bagavathi*. *Ponthi*, is a short iron rod, is believed as, the weapon of the deity *gulikan*. It is kept in the house of the *karanavar*. It is used only during the time of festivals.

There is a popular myth associated with origin of name of the community as how the people recollect it. Choondal (2003) says that there was a conflict between *eleri* and *mothali* in Nilamboor. At last *eleri* beaten (*thachu) mothali*. As *mothali* is superior in position by fear of punishment *eleri* with his family and relatives escaped to Wayanad. *Elery* and *mothali* are the equivalent terms for *moopan* and *lepan* in Wayanad. In Thachanadan Moopan dialect beaten refers *thachu*. It is belived by the people thus they got the name Thachanadan.

They believe in supreme deity called *karivilli kariyathan*. They also believe in the ancestral spirits. It is believed that ancestors are the helpers of *karivilli kariyathan*. Thachanadan Moopan are the descendents of these ancestral spirits. They have ancestral spirits on *padi* and *chali* level. The ancestral spirits of *padi* is called *kurikkal* and *chali* is called *muthachi*. Depends up on the ancestral spirits they divided the 36 *padi* and 101 *chali* in to groups. They believe that ancestral spirits resides in the *kanayam*. *Kanayam*, also as the symbol of authority, found in *moopan*, *lepan*, and *chali thekkanam*'s house, handed over generation after generation. It is dangled in the corner of the room along with peacock feathers, usually the *kanayam* is kept on the deer horn and that is tied in the roof. The room, where the *kanayam* is kept, is known as *Karanavastanam*. Each *padi* and *chali* has their own *kanayam*. *Tharavadu kanayam*, the residence of *kurikal* (the male ancestral spirits) will not taken outside the boundary of that *tharavadu*, and *chali kanayam* is shifted to the place of the *chali thekkanam* as the position is held on the elderly basis, and there is no restriction in the movement of *chali kanayam*. Their other main deities are *bagavathi* and *gulikan*. *Gulikan* always possess with weapon called *ponthi*, which is a short iron rod. *Gulikan* is considered as the *kavalkaran* (watcher) of the *kunnu* (hill). *Bagvathi* is the Goddesses of Thachanadan Moopan. *Bagavathi* also exists in different forms and names such as *cheriya bagavathi*, *valiya bagavathi*, *choorukundu bagavathi* etc. *Bagavathi* is also called *thamburaty*. Sword is the weapon of *bagavathi* and *pattu* is the cloth of *bagavathi*. *Mariamman* is considered as the goddess of health. It is believed that the diseases like smallpox and mesles are easily cured by visiting and praying *mariamman*.

Thachanadan Moopan practicing taboos, regarding the prohibition of marriage with in ones own *chali* or *padi*, death of a person or the pollution associated with women during the period of menstruation, delivery etc. They also believe in the omens and evil eye. They are saying that the man or women who possess these eyes can bring ruin to a person, destroy his household members, domestic animals, crops and houses. An example for omen is, if a person wakes up and if she or he happens to see mirror, a pot full of water or lamp is considered to be lucky for that person. Psychologically by see is a pot full of water in the morning itself one may get pleasure to the mind and then get energetic.

Their important deities are *karivillykariyathan, bagavathi, gulikan* and ancestral spirits. The idol of *gulikan* is in the *moopan's* house and in *kaavu* (sacred grove) too. Before each and every hunt, the people go and seek permission of the *gulikan* and also they worship it for a good hunt too. There are some sacred performances related with *gulikan* especially *narukku vekkuka* ceremony. *Bagvathi* is the Goddess of Thachanadan Moopan. *Bagavathi* also exists in different forms and names such as *cheriya bagavathi, valiya bagavathi, choorukundu bagavathi* etc. *Bagavathi* is also called *thamburaty*. Sword is the weapon of *bagavathi* and *pattu* is the cloth of *bagavathi*

There is a myth about ancestral spirits of Thachanadan Moopan. It is believed that ancestors are the helpers of *karivilli kariyathan*. Thachanadan Moopan are the descendents of these ancestral spirits. As per the myth, *muthan* and *muthi* have six daughters and seven sons. The *muthi* and six daughters form the seven *muthachi* of 101 *chali* (lineage) and the seven sons are the *kurikkal* of 36 *padi* (clan). Based on this *muthachi* and *kurikkal,* the *padi* and *chali* divisions have been formed. They have the belief that the head part of the *muthan* has been severed in a war and he became two half *kurikkals* and become a stone. Thus, he has come to be known as *aravayavan* who is also called *muthappan*. He has the supreme position among the ancestral spirits.

Sacred groves contains few trees, such as *kaatu chembakam* (Michelia champaca), *Pala* (Alstonia scholaris), *poomaram* (Delonix regia), banyan tree, neem tree, *poola* (Bombax ceiba) and other local wild trees are also found there. The important rituals taking place in the *kaavu* is during the time of *uthsavam*. It begins with the *pooja* to all gods, then the oracle of every gods and deities will come. *karpa pooja, kozhiyarakkal, kanalattam*. Are the rituals they are performing in the *kaavu*. *Moopan* and *lepan* are the important religious functionaries. *Moopan* and *lepan* had multifarious works. *Moopan* is the head of the *tharavadu* and *lepan* is his assistant and deputy. Thus *moopan* and *lepan* have important role in the social, political and religious matters. *Moopan* performs all sorts of religious ceremonies; he led the important events of social and economic significance. And he acts as the doctor, who identifies the spirits responsible for causing diseases and prescribes the nature of sacrifices to be made. As a spiritual guide he secures blessing of the spirits by propitiating them time to time. In olden days people paid to him in the form of vegetables and ornaments. At present they pay in both cash and kind.

Velichapadu has an important position in the ritual and related ceremonies of Thachanadan Moopan. *Velichapadu* acts as an intermediary between God and ordinary people. The person who gets *darshanam,* ie the possession of the God, ancestral spirits or dead persons is the *velichapadu* on each occasion. Both male and female persons get *darshanam* (possession). All the persons, whom ever able to speak the matter thoroughly and clearly could beceome *velichapadu.* Seven or twenty one days of *noyamb* (fasting) is taken to become a *velichapadu. Velichapadu* has several roles. The *velichapadu* is also called during *adiyanthiram* to solve the problems related to death, during the selection of next *karanavar, etc.* When they go for hunting, *velichapadu* of *gulikan* is called and asked about the hunting. Each and every *tharavadu* has its own members to perform *velichapadu.* If there is no one to perform the role they take from other families by giving money.

Thachanadan Moopan practice sorcery and witchcraft. The techniques on understanding about magic, and also techniques about ethno-medicine preserved by some specialists and it was not open to public. Knowledge in the magical practices is accessible only to a few selected persons among them and they could keep them as secret and treat them as most valuable treasure. This secret knowledge about medicinal plants and magical rites are always transferred orally through generations. They are doing magico- religious practices mainly to cure the diseases. Their sorcery is called *odiyan pani.* The old people especially those who have knowledge about medicine are called as *chakran* or *chakrathi* in the language of Thachanadan Moopan. *Kandam vekuka* is one of the magico-religious practices to find out the diseases. This is performed by *chakruthi* or *chakran,* by using *manthras* and they use herbal medicines to treat. If the disease is minor, they only give the charmed water. Sometime they give thread to wear in the body. *Chakruthi or chakran* measures the hand of the diseased person, from ankle to finger tip by spreading her hand thumb to point length. While measuring, they also chant *manthras*. If the measurement is not completed in the hand of the person, the person would not have any disease. If the measuring length is less than the hand, the disease must be serious. If the length ends in the palm, it is believed that it happens due to the dissatisfaction of the deity.

Their important performances are *chaalileoottu, kambakuthukallynam,* ritual performing during the selection of new *karanavar, karpa pooja, kallivettal,* ceremony related to *kanayam,* when it fell down, *muttu arackuka* and *kathiretukkal chatangu.* Apart from this, they are playing some folk plays related to the sacred performances such as *kolkali, vattakali* etc.

The religious behavior of the community is changing. It is mainly because of the process of acculturation and cultural contact etc. The major change happened religious system is acceptence of alien faiths. As a Scheduled Tribe traditionally they have their own belief system and practices as described earlier. But due to the contact with the main stream people, missionaries and mass media etc. the processes of hinduisation and christianization is increasing day by day. In the case of hinduisation nobody is inspiring or forcing them to accept Hindu Gods and Goddesses, instead some factors such as to come upward in the social stratum, and to be equal with the other plains people they have to imitate them because they are surrounded by the vast environment of Hinduism, which often belittles tribal way of life. There is the inferiority complexion created in their mind that they are worshiping the sticks (*kanayam*) is also one of the factor that compelled them to accept the higher caste Gods and their manner of worshipping. Hindu Gods appear in the houses through wall calenders and pictures. Belief in the witchcraft and sorcery is declining but belief in the ancestral spirits, and taboos are not much declined. Education, economic security and availability of modern medical facilities are the breaking factors of age old beliefs. Nowadays they started to construct small temples. And they also started worshiping in a manner similar to that of Brahminical tradition by fixing a *poojari* (a person from a *namboothiri* caste to perform rituals) to carry out sacredotal functions. Thus the role of *moopan* and *lepan* as religious functionaries is declining.

The missionaries come to villages and preaching about Jesus Christ. some of them are taking to christianity simply because of their faith in the Jesus Christ. In many cases the pastor pray for the people who ever is with disease, family and personal problems. When these people found that these prayers worked in their life automatically, they are embracing Christianity. This makes others to believe that Christianity as real path. Missioneries are also helping during the marriage occasion and house construction, if the family is not financially capable. Education another factor, due to the close contact with the Christian community they have realized the importance of education to their children. Even though the govt. providing stipends and all it's not enough for a family for the whole year. Thus missionaries giving of new dress, books etc and encourage them to go to the school. They are also giving medicines through medical camps, not only to the converted but to all people whomever is in need.

The traditional Thachanadan Moopans say that they do not maintain any contact with those converted to Christianity. They are not allowed to participate in any of the life cycle rituals of Thachanadan Moopan. They treat them as another group. The converted creating themselves as new endogamic group by marrying with in the penthacostals. But in such cases there is no geographical boundary. They can marry any penthacostal any where in the state. It is also believed that Christianized people not at all worshiping and propitiating the ancestral spirits and supernatural. They are not keeping any purity concept. Thus they may get the wrath of the god and also those that interact with them. Thus traditional people are keeping distance with the Christian Thachanadan Moopan.

Thus after joining to Christianity they are completely leaving the traditional practices and beliefs. But while adopting Hinduism they are not leaving the traditional practices fully.

Conclusion

Thachanadan Moopan traditionally believes in the supernatural powers spirits and the supreme God. Still now they are observing some of the taboos and customs.

While they transfer to Christianity they are leaving all the traditional beliefs and practices. Because Christianity as their religion they are moving to create a new group as in the name of Christianized tribal, but few in number. But those who are accepting Hinduism are not at all leaving their traditional practices, rather the tribal beliefs and hindu practices are fusing togather Thus on the basis of religion Thachanadan Moopan are divided in to two distinct groups that are Christianized and Hinduised. The traditional tribal group could not keep its separate identity as the marriage between them and those hinduised is very thin and have both of them are amalgamated.

REFERENCES

Aleaz, K P., 2002. A Tribal Theology From A Tribal World – View. *IJT.* 44(2):20-30.

Bagabati, C., 1998. *Indegenous faiths and practices of the tribes of Arunachal Pradesh.* New Delhi: Rawat Publications.

Barnbas, A.P., 1967. *Social change in north Indian village.* New Delhi: Indian Institute of Public administration.

Birx, J., (Edt) 2006. *Encyclopaedia of Anthropology Vol 5.* U.K: Sage Publications.

Bisht, B.S., 2001. *Ethnography of a Tribe: study of Anwals of Uttarakhand Himalaya.* Jaipur: Rawat Publications.

Boyer, P and Brian Bergstrom. 2008. Evolutionery perspective on religion. *Annual review of Anthropology.* 37:111-130.

Chaudhari, S K., 2004. *Understanding tribal religion.* New Delhi: Mittal Publication.

Chettiar, 2002. *Folklore of Tamil Nadu*. New Delhi: National Book Trust.

Choondal, C., 1991. *Karuthakalakal (Malayalam)*. New Delhi: Common Wealth Publications.

Choondal, C., 2003. *Janajeevithavum kalakalum (Malayalam)*. Kannur: Kerala Folklore Academy.

Choudhary, S. K., 2004. *Tribal identity continuity an changes among the KJoudhs of Orissa*. New Delhi: Rawat Publications.

Comaroff, J and John Comaroff. 1991. *Of Revelation and Revolution: Christianity, Colonialism, and Consciousness in South Africa - Vol. 1*. London: The university of Chicago press.

D'Souza, L., 2005. *The Sociology of religion: A historical review*. New Delhi: Rawat Publication.

Dash, K.N, 2005. *An invitation to social and cultural anthropology*. New Delhi: Atlantic Publishers.

Davis, J., 1982. *Religious experience reader in Anthropology*. New York: Brace Jovanovich.

Dawar, J L., 2003. *Cultural identity of North East India: Movement for cultural identity among Adis of Arunachal Pradesh*. New Delhi: Commonwealth publications.

Debashish, D., 2003. *Ecology and Rituals in Tribal areas*. New Delhi: Rawat Publications.

Douglas, M., 1966. *Purity and danger: An analysis of concepts of pollution and taboo*. London: Routledge

Eller, J D., 2007. *Anthropology of religion.* New York: Routledge Publication.

Ellwood, C. A., 1913. The social function of religion. *The American Journal of Sociology.* (19): 289-307.

Frazer, J., 1958. *The Golden Bough.* London.

Gennep, A V., 1906. *The Rites of Passage.* London: Routledge.

Goode, W. J., 1951. *Religion among Primitive.* Glencoe, Ill : Free Press.

Goody, J., 1962. *Death, property and the ancestors: A study of the mortuary customs of the LoDagaa of West Africa.* Stanford: Stanford University Press.

Hendry, J., 1999. *An Introduction to Social Anthropology-Other peoples World.* New York: Palgrave.

Horton, P.B. and Hunt, C.H. 1960. *Sociology.* New York: Mac Graw Hill.

Jain, P.C., 1995. *Christianity Ideology and social change among tribals: A case study of Bhils of Rajput.* New Delhi: Rawat Publications.

Jain, S., 2004. *Adi Deo Arya Devata- A Panoramic view of tribal Hindhu Cultural Inference.* New Delhi: Rawat Publications

Kattakayam, J J., 1983. *Social structure and change among the tribals.* BR Publishing Corporation: New Delhi.

Kim, S. C. H., 2003. *In search if identity: Debates on religiois conversion in India.* New Delhi: Oxford University press.

Kottak, C P., 1987. *Anthropology- The exploration of human diversity,* New York: Random House.

Kottak, Conrad, and Kathryn A. Koazitis. 2002. *On being different: Diversity and multiculturalism in the North American Mainstream.* Boston: McGraw-Hill.

Mac Lennan, S. F. 1922. Religion and Anthropology. *The Journal of Religion,* 2(6): 600-615

Mair, L P., 1971. *Anthropology and social change.* UK: The athlone press.

Majumdar, D.N. and Madan. 1986. *An introduction to social anthropology.* Bombay: Asia publishing house.

Maralusiddiah, H.M., 2002. Thachanad Moopan. In. *People of India: Kerala Vol xxvii.* K.S. Singh Eds. New Delhi: Anthropological Survey of India.

Martindale, D., 1962. *Social life and cultural life.* New York: Sterling publishers.

Menon, M., 2003. Tribal religion and Hindu cult: Case studies from South India. In. *Culture, Religion and Philosophy.* N.K Das. Eds. New Delhi. Rawat Publications.

Mesquitela, L., 1987. *Fetishism.Encyclopedia of Religion.* New York: Mac Milan Publishing Company.

Miller, B., 1999. *Cultural anthropology* New York: Peorson Publications.

Miller, Mary and Karl Taube. 1993. *The god's and symbols of ancient Mexico and the Maya.* Newyork: Thames and Hudson.

Mishra, N., 2004. *Tribal culture in India.* New Delhi: Kalpaz publications.

Moore. W. E., 1968. *Social change.* New Delhi: Prentice- Hall of India.

Nair, J., 2008. *Encyclopedia of social sciences.* New Delhi: Pentagon Press.

Nordskog, J E., 1960. *Special change.* New York: Mc Graw Hill book co.

Pathania, R and Pawan Pathania. 2008. Religious Beliefs among Tribal of Himachal Pradesh. *Anthropologist,* 10(2):143-145

Pohlong, B., 2004. *Culture and religion a conceptual study.* New York. Mittal publications.

Robinson, R., 1998. *Conversion continuity and change.* New Delhi: sage publications

Sahay, K N., 1998. *Dynamics and dimensions of tribal societies.* Common Wealth Publishers: New Delhi

Seul, J R., 1999. Ours is the way of God': Religion, identity, and intergroup conflict *Journal of Peace Research,* 36(5) 553-569

Sharma, M. S., 2001. *Encyclopedic dictionery of religion and ethics.* New Delhi: Mohit Publications.

Sharma, Uma Kanta and and Shyamanta Pegu. 2011. Ethnobotany of religious and supernatural beliefs of the Mising tribes of Assam with special reference to the 'Dobur Uie'. *Journal of Ethnobiology and Ethnomedicine* 7(16): 1-13.

Sholaparker, G.R., 1990. *Religious rites and festivals in India.* New Delhi: Bharathiya vidya prakasan.

Singh, K.S., 2003. Hinduism and Tribal Religion: An Anthropological Perspective on interaction. In. *Culture, Religion and Philosophy* N.K Das (Eds) New Delhi: Rawat Publications.

Singh, R., 2000. *Tribal beliefs and practices and insurrections.* New Delhi. Anmol publications.

Srinivas, M.N., 1952. *Social change in modern India.* Bombay: Orient Longman.

Srivastava, A., 2008. *Social Anthropology.* New Delhi: DFominent publications.

Srivastava, M., 2007. The sacred complex of Munda. *Anthropologist.* 327-330.

Sundar, N., 2001. Religion and Culture in Bastar: The politics of conversion. *Eastern Anthropologist.* 53(34):

Troisy, J. 2000. *Tribal religion religious beliefs and practices among the Santhal.* New Delhi: Manohar Publications.

Turner, V W., 1961. *Ndembu divination: Its symbolism and techniques.* New York: Humanities Press.

Tylor, E.B., 1871. *Primitive Culture: Researches in to the development of mythology, philosophy, religion, language, art and customs, Vol 2.* London: J Murrary.

Tylor, E.B., 2002. Animism In. *Basic elements of tribal religion.* S.M. Channa.(Eds) New Delhi: Cosmo publications.

Upadhyay and Gaya Pandey., 1993. *History of anthropological thought.* New Delhi: Concept publishing Company.

V.P, S., 2008. *Lifecycle rituals of Thachanadan Moopan.* Unpublished thesis submitted in the department of Anthropology, Kannur University, Palayad campus.

VanPool, C S., 2003. The shaman priest of the Casas Grandes region, Chihuahua, Mexico. *American antiquity,* 68 (4): 696-717.

Vasudeva, P., 1976. *Social change.* New Delhi: Sterling Publication.

Vidhyarthi, L.P and Rai, 1983. *Tribal culture of India.* New Delhi: Concept publishing company.

Vidhyarthi, L.P., 1963. *The Maler- A study in nature – man –spirit complex of a hill tribe.* Culcutta: culcutta bookland.

Vitebsky, P., 2001. *Shamanism.* Oklahoma: University of oklahoma press.

Walker, A. R., 1998. *Todas people of south India between tradition and modernity.* New Delhi: B.R publishing co-op Ltd.

Weber, M., 1963. *The Sociology of Religion.* Transl. E. Fischoff. Boston. Beacon.

Yinger, M., 1957. *Religion Society and the Individual: An introduction to the Sociology of religion.* Macmilan: Newyork.

APPENDIX OF LOCAL TERMS

Bgavathi	One of the deity
Chakruthi/chakran	Medicine Man/women
Chali Thekkanam	Head of the Clan
Chunnambu	Calcium hydroxide
Dakshina	Offering
Darshanam	Possession
Gulikan	One of the deity
Janmi	Land lord
Kaatu Chembakam	A tree (Michelia champaca)
Kadakam	Aboard of the deity
Kalpana	Order
Kanayam	Religious symbol
Kandam vekuka	A method of diagnosis
Karanavastanam	The place where
Kari	Fuel wood powder
Karimi and manakam	Religious functionaries
Karinkutty	A deity

KarivilliKariyathan	The supreme God believed to be the incarnation of Shiva and Parvathy
Karukkapullu	A type of grass
Kathiretuckal chatangu	Harvesting ceremony
kathukuthu kallyanam	Ear-boring ceremony
Kavalkaran	Watcher
Kavu	Sacred grove
kolkali adiyanthirakal/ Vattakali	Folk plays
Kulam/chali	Matrilineal descent group
Kurikkal	Ancestral spirit of Pady
Lord Ayyappa	God of Hindu
Makkalu	Children
Malar	Popped rice
Mandapam	The platform made of mud for worshipping
Marumakkathayam	A family consisting of mother and children living with the maternal Uncle
Moopan/ Leppan	Political head of the tharavadu
Muthachi	Ancestral spirit of chali
Naakkila	Plantains leaf
Nair	A caste group
Naruk	Pieces
Odi vekkuka	Black magic
Odiyan pani/	
Padi and kunnu	Patrilineal descent group

Pala	A tree (Alstonia scholaris)
Pattar	A caste group
Pettichi	Midwife
Ponthi	Iron stick used by the Gulikan
Poomaram	A tree (delonix regia)
Tharavadu, Utsavam	Festival
Velichappadu	Oracle

Photographs

SACRED OBJECTS

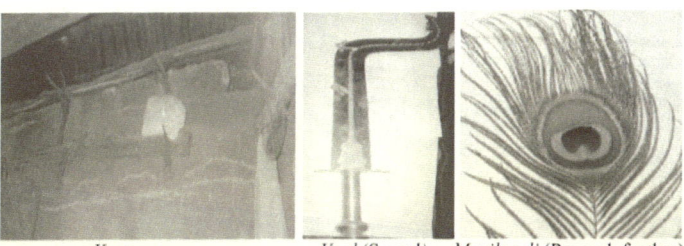

Kaanayam   *Vaal* (Sword)   *Mayilpeeli* (Peacock feather)

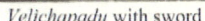
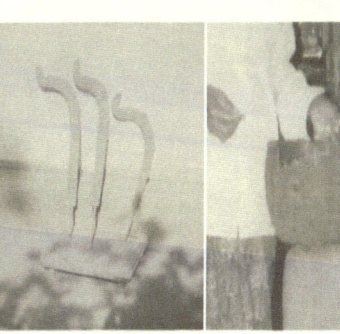

Velichapadu with sword   Sword and *kooda* kept in *Karanavastanam*

Kuthuvilikku in *kaavu*

SACRED GEOGRAPHY AND SACRED CENTRES

Sacred geography and worshipping centers (*Kaavu*)

SACRED PERFORMANCES

Kolkali – The folk play *Narukku vekkuka* (A ritual)

SACRED SPECIALISTS

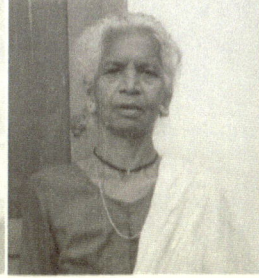

Velichapadu   *Chakruthi* (Medicine women)

Moopan, Moopathi and family members

CHANGING BELIEF SYSTEM

Photographs of Hindhu Gods and Goddesses on the wall   A Penthacostal church

INDEX

www.ingramcontent.com/pod-product-compliance
Lightning Source LLC
Chambersburg PA
CBHW020901310526
45786CB00018B/868